I am dedicating this book to Linda, my wife and the anchor that helped get me through an incredibly difficult trial and to our wonderful children and grandchildren with the hope that this might help them get through challenging times in their lives.

And what would a book from Dad and "Grumpa" be without one of his favorite quotes?

"Life is tough! And your point is?"

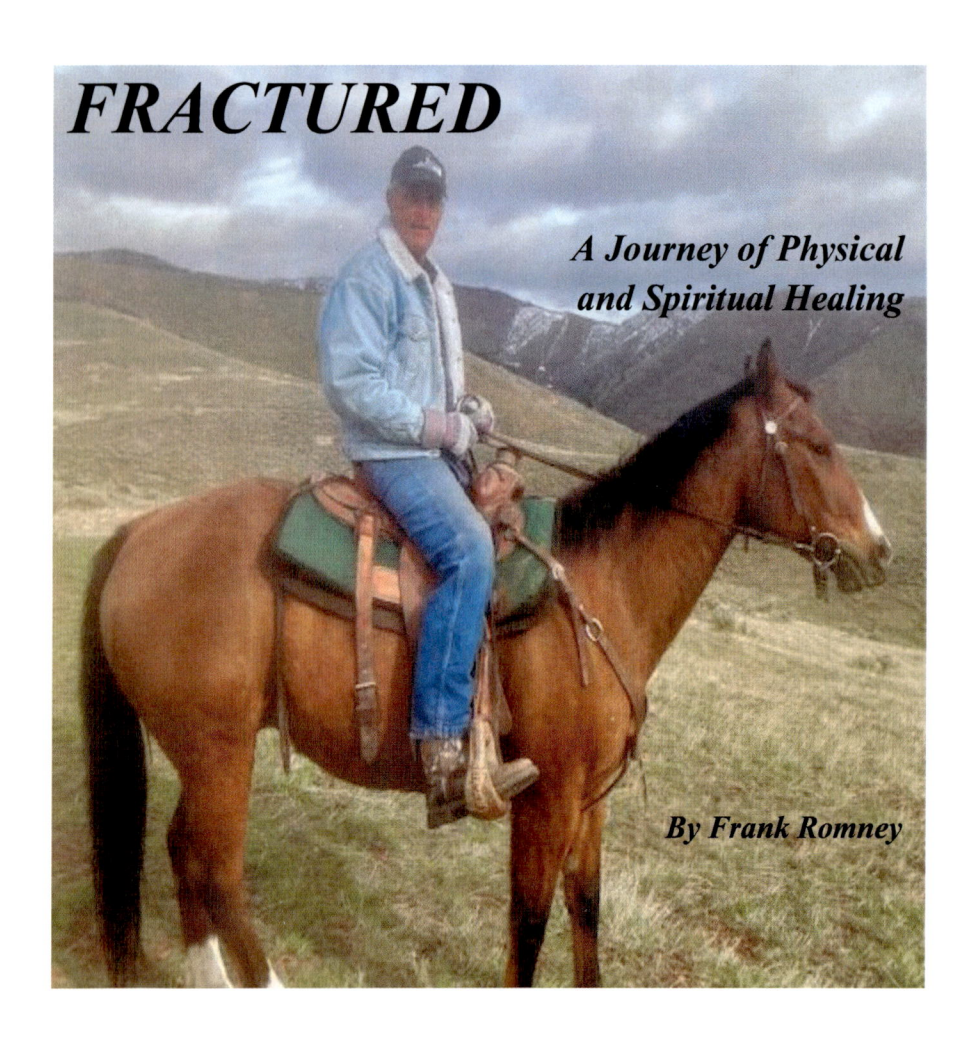

FRACTURED

A Journey of Physical and Spiritual Healing

By Frank Romney

Table of Contents

Prologue i

Chapter 1 Turmoil 1

Chapter 2 Fractured 6

Chapter 3 Surgery 17

Chapter 4 Storm After the Calm 21

Chapter 5 Be Still My Soul 39

Chapter 6 "It's Old News" 46

Chapter 7 If Thou Wouldst Have a Blessing of Me…..........50

Chapter 8 Too Many Blessings? 57

Chapter 9 Ministering Angels 65

Chapter 10 Don't Look Down.. 73

Epilogue 81

Prologue

"Anger, if not restrained, is frequently more [destructive] than the injury that provokes it." [1]

I never experienced anger at what happened to me, never asked why me nor have I felt anger towards the surgeon and the surgery that left me with excruciating pain and nerve damage. I have felt much gratitude as I kept a daily journal and recorded the many miracles, answered prayers and ministering of friends, acquaintances and even strangers throughout this experience. Many of the journal entries were positive and focused on the blessings I was receiving while going through an exceedingly hard challenge. There were also those that contained the painful, lonely, and dark moments I experienced as I was pushed to the edge of my faith emotionally, physically, and spiritually.

After sharing some of my experiences with a few friends, church members and some of my former patients that came to visit me in the care center, including the struggles and the many small miracles and blessings I had received along the way, several of them were surprised with my positive attitude and told me I had to write a book to help others. After having been encouraged several times to write this story, I concluded that if sharing my experience could help others experiencing difficult trials then I should do it.

 While recuperating in the care facility, a former patient was admitted after having had back fusion surgery. We would frequently both be in the physical therapy gym at the same time. Unfortunately for

i

her she was exposed to all my jokes. I was usually upbeat in the therapy sessions. I was so happy to be moving forward and not just lying around in bed and my attitude encouraged her to keep trying. Her surgery left her deconditioned and in a lot of pain. She had a difficult time trying to heal and keep moving forward. I remember one day in particular, months after our shared time in the care center, she came into my physical therapy clinic for treatment and was having a really hard day. The pain in her back and right leg was intense and she was very discouraged. As I worked on her, she looked at me and said, "Hurry and finish your book. I need to read it to help me get through this."

One night, before going to sleep, I started reading the book Silent Souls Weeping by Jane Clayson Johnson. One of the first things I read inspired me to keep working on my book. She wrote, that at times, while writing her book that, "I couldn't do it justice. But then I would talk to someone else and see their eyes light up when I mentioned the book I was writing and what I hoped it could do. I would take another step forward." [2]

I turned off the light and went to sleep. I woke up at 2:45 in the morning and started putting down these thoughts. I am not a professional writer, but I pray that as you read this story you will feel a quiet, heavenly assurance that you are not alone and that you can endure and grow through difficult challenges and trials in your life.

Trust in the Lord with all thine heart; and lean not unto thine own understanding. In all thy ways acknowledge him, and he shall direct thy paths.

(Proverbs 3:5-6)

Notes

1 Seneca, in Tryon Edwards, *A Dictionary of Thoughts* (1891), 21.

2 Silent Souls Weeping, Jane Clayson, p. 11-12

1

Turmoil

"This know also, that in the last days perilous times shall come. For men shall be lovers of their own selves, covetous, boasters, proud, blasphemers, disobedient to parents, unthankful, unholy, without natural affection, trucebreakers, false accusers, incontinent, fierce, despisers of those that are good, traitors, heady, high minded, lovers of pleasures more than lovers of God; Having a form of godliness, but denying the power thereof: from such turn away." (2 Timothy 3:1-5)

What a year it had been so far. President Trump lost the election amid cries of voter ballot tampering and fraud. There were riots at the capitol building in Washington D.C. Major cities such as Seattle, Washington and Portland, Oregon were trying to recover from widespread rioting, looting, violence, and economically as more and more businesses left these cities or states. Society struggled with shrinking police departments after labeling the police as "the bad guys" and defunding their departments, severely restricting their ability to enforce the law.

The news and social media glorified criminal activity. Platforms such as Facebook and Twitter censored people that expressed conservative ideas and philosophies, limiting freedom of speech. They also promoted right as being wrong and wrong as being right. If you stood up for morals, you were labeled as biased and judgmental, but if you lived by the motto that "anything goes" and "there is no wrong," then you were seen as enlightened. If you stood to sing the national anthem or say the Pledge of Allegiance, you were labeled a racist. It seemed that the Black Lives Matter movement that was supposedly promoting social equality was dividing the country and not promoting any positive actions. Shoplifting was legalized in California.

With all this turmoil and strife, it was no wonder that people were leaving religion, indulging in self-pleasures and the pursuit of wealth, at any cost. The family unit was under attack. Parents were taking their newborn infants home from the hospital without an assigned gender and were choosing to let their children decide which gender they are.

The Covid Pandemic with all its controversial coverage and politicization was dividing the country both health-wise and psychologically. If you got the Covid vaccination you were labeled as "sheeple," implying that you hadn't put any thought into the decision but followed along like a mindless sheep. If you chose not to get the vaccination, you were labeled as an uncaring rebel.

Just for fun, we can add the wars and rumors of wars, national and international terrorism, extreme weather, political unrest, corruption, and a federal government that was incentivizing people to stay home from work.

Many businesses closed their doors or just limped along because they couldn't find people willing to work. Gas prices were increasing rapidly, construction materials were skyrocketing, and grocery prices climbed higher weekly. The borders were being overrun by illegal immigrants in record numbers. Need I go on?

On a lighter note, there were the covid masks. As a member of a newly called Young Single Adult bishopric, in the Church of Jesus Christ of Latter-day Saints, I was often frustrated trying to learn the names of members of our congregation, when all I could see was their eyes. I made mental images of what I thought they looked like and found I was wrong when I eventually saw their faces uncovered. It was like hearing the voice of a radio personality. If you are like me, you create an image in your mind, based on their radio voice, of what they look like and, when you see them, they don't look anything like you imagined.

I don't want you to think I am a pessimist because the reality is, at least in my small world, most people still have good morals, and they care about their families, neighbors, and friends. Religion is still important to many, as is serving others. Not everyone is racist, bigoted, or prejudiced. In my physical therapy clinic, I treat people of all races and socioeconomic classes, and they all receive the same treatment.

Why did I bring up all these events, the social unrest and the moral challenges facing our society this year? There is not a day that goes by that most or all of us don't discuss one or more of these topics with co-workers, family, or friends. Even if we don't discuss what is going on in society and the world, we are inundated with opinions and negative stories in the news and social media, and they are available 24 hours a day. This was the world as I perceived it in May of 2021.

On a more personal level, have you ever noticed that when there is some significant event in your life, be it an injury, illness, or some other trial, that your life comes to a stop and all the worldly chaos suddenly fades into the background? Sometimes in life we are faced with what can seem to be an overwhelming challenge or trial, illness or injury, disease or even death. When this happens, the noise and distractions and problems of society quickly fade into the background and your world becomes much smaller and can at times seem much lonelier as you are isolated from the world and many of those you associate with. We all have or will experience this at some time in our lives, either personally or with someone that is central to our life.

May 22, 2021, was one of those times in my life. One moment life was good, I was doing one of my favorite things in life with my wife and friends and in a matter of seconds, everything changed. My life came to a sudden and unexpected halt. The world continued with business as usual as my wife, Linda, sitting on an emergency room chair and me lying on an emergency room bed, received the news from the doctor that I had fractured my pelvis in three places and that I wouldn't be going home that night. Little did we know what challenges and struggles were ahead of us and what this was going to do to our lives.

2

Fractured

"In this place I got mixed up with plowing, sowing, reaping, haymaking, and so forth, and have indelibly impressed on my mind some of my first mishaps in horsemanship in the shape of sundry curious evolutions between horses' backs and terra firma." [1]

As a physical therapist for 34 years, I have worked on patients with a variety of injuries. Personally, I have experienced my own fair share of injuries, some minor and some significant. This injury has, by far, been the most severe injury and most physically, mentally, spiritually, and financially challenging injury of my life. Spiritually it has pushed me to the edge of the cliff of faith.

In the book, Faith Is Not Blind, Bruce C. Hafen and Marie K. Hafen, quote Elder Neal A. Maxwell, an apostle in the Church of Jesus Christ of Latter-day Saints, after he was diagnosed with cancer. "When the Lord takes us "to the very edge of our faith; [and] we teeter at the edge of our trust [in] a form of learning as it is administered at the hands of a loving father." [2] This summed up my feelings.

I love all things related to horses. I enjoy watching them, being around them, feeding them, brushing them, saddling them, and of course riding them. When I am around horses, the stresses of life seem to melt away. I remember one event that really describes what horses have come to mean in my life.

In May of 2018, my father, who was 90 years old, had moderate dementia. He also had problems with a small esophagus. One day, because of his small esophagus, he choked on some food at mealtime. This was not the first time this had happened. This time, however, it was different. After he got past the choking episode, he stopped eating. Over the next 6-7 days he didn't eat or drink. My sisters and my wife and I took turns sitting with him and my mother, sometimes just listening and counting his breaths and watching for signs of him waking up. He was put on hospice care, and they helped us get through his last week of life. On the seventh day, I was at work when I got the phone call letting me know that he had passed away quietly in the room he and my mother shared in an assisted living center. Another one of those moments, when the noise and distractions and problems of society quickly faded into the background, as our father's death became the center of our family focus.

Several days after he passed away, our good friends, Blaine, and Diane, invited us to go horseback riding. They had no idea that my father had passed away. I am one that often keeps things to myself, and this was one of those times. We met them up in Mountain Green at their horse property. We went to the different pastures, put harnesses on the horses, led them back and then tied them up to the hitching posts. After brushing them we threw on the saddle blankets and saddles, cinched them down tight, put on their bridles and proceeded to enjoy a wonderful ride through the countryside on the horses. It was a peaceful, sunny afternoon. I was in the back as we rode along in single file. My wife Linda, Diane and Blaine were having a conversation but for the most part I listened but didn't talk much.

As I rode along, I felt the sun on my face and stared off to the west at the eastern slopes of the beautiful Wasatch mountains. Between the sunshine, listening to the quiet conversation of Linda, Diane and Blaine, the beautiful scenery, and the rhythm of my horse walking along, I became lost in quiet, contemplative thought. The pain and sadness melted away, replaced by a deep sense of peace. I believe animals can sense our feelings and my horse could sense mine that day. I was able to let him have his head, let the reins hang slack in my hand as he followed the other horses, almost as if he felt my pain and took over, allowing me to get lost in my thoughts and feelings. I love all things related to horses and Diane and Blaine who have always generously shared their horses with us.

Fractured

Saturday, May 22, 2021, I woke up early. Our friends had invited us to go horseback riding and I was excited. We arrived at Mountain Green at their horse property. It was a beautiful, sunny spring morning. Perfect conditions for riding the horses. We followed our usual routine. We went to the different pastures, harnessed the horses, led them back to the hitching posts, brushed and saddled them. As usual, Blaine asked me which horse I wanted to ride, and I chose Jet. He was a younger horse, and I had ridden him many times in the past. He was friskier than the other horses, which I liked, because it challenged my average riding skills, which I was always trying to improve. For the next hour or so we walked, trotted, and loped around the field enjoying conversation and our shared love of horses. Occasionally, I would trot over to Linda to see how she was doing. That day, as I rode Jet, he would occasionally toss his head down and to one side. It would throw my balance off a little, but I was able to grab the saddle horn and center myself in the saddle. As we were coming to the end of our ride, I spurred my horse for one more trip across the field. Partway across the field he tossed his head down and to one side and then did it again towards the other side in quick succession. Without warning I found myself out of the saddle, in the air, parallel to his side and looking at my left foot in the stirrup.

He hadn't bucked but those two quick, unexpected head and shoulder movements had unseated me before I could grab the saddle horn. My thoughts went into slow motion as I first thought, "I'm falling off my horse," and then looked at my left foot still in the stirrup and thought, "I hope my foot comes out of the stirrup so that I don't get dragged by the horse."

I hit the ground hard, landing on my left side. After the impact, time sped up again. The wind had been knocked out of me. My left arm was pinned underneath my side, and I felt a sharp pain where my ribs were in contact with my elbow. I wondered if I had broken my ribs. Besides the pain in my ribs, I felt pain in my lower back. I had had a lumbar discectomy a year before, and my first concern was that I had damaged my back again. I just lay there, trying to relax and catch my breath. Gradually, I caught my breath, and the rib pain started to ease as did the lower back pain. It was then that I became aware of pain in my left groin and right buttocks. Linda and Blaine rode up to me and asked if I was okay. I told them I just needed a few minutes. I rolled over onto my stomach and then pushed up onto my hands and knees with the intent of standing up. I made it up onto my right knee. As I tried to bring my left knee and foot forward so that I could push up on the leg and stand up, I felt a very sharp pain in my left groin. It was painful enough that it forced me back down onto my hands and knees. It was then that Linda rode over to where our vehicle was parked, climbed in, and drove our vehicle out into the field where I had fallen. With the help of Linda and Blaine, I was able to stand up on my right leg. I couldn't tolerate any weight on my left leg, because of the intense groin pain. They helped me sit down on the seat and then lifted my left leg into the vehicle. Linda slowly drove us back to where the other vehicles were parked. Diane got me a cold rag and a drink, and I reclined the seat and went into shock. After a few minutes, the shock faded. We all had a discussion as to what I should do. Blaine tried calling his son-in-law, who is a physician, to see if he could come over and do a portable ultrasound. His son-in-law didn't answer, and we decided I ought to go to the emergency room. Being an optimist, or maybe in this case someone in complete denial, I talked Linda into driving over to my physical therapy clinic, grabbing a pair of crutches and then taking me home. I thought that if I could rest and let some time pass that I would be all right. I was thinking it was probably just a bad groin strain.

After picking up crutches from my clinic, Linda drove us home. I could feel every bump in the road. Every time we went around a corner it caused my weight to shift and increased the pain. I would brace myself with my arms on the console and armrest of the door and try and take pressure off my pelvis. As she turned into our driveway, the bump as we crossed the curb cutout about did me in. We pulled up to the house and Linda drove into the garage and shut off the engine. She grabbed the pair of crutches from the back seat and opened my door. I was able to swing my right leg out but needed help moving the left leg. With both feet on the ground and Linda's hand steadying me, I stood up putting all my weight on the right leg, using the crutches for balance and support. At first, I couldn't move forward. I tried to lift my left foot and swing my leg, but the pain was so intense I couldn't move my leg. I then found that if I moved the crutch tips forward twelve inches, I could raise up on the toes of my right foot and then let the left leg swing forward. It was painful but manageable. I made my way to the bottom of the twelve steps leading up into the house. There was no way I could go up the stairs facing forward because I couldn't swing the left leg forward let alone lift the foot up onto the step. After a minute, an idea came to mind. I decided to go backwards up the stairs. I found that I could place my hands on the handrails on both sides of the stairs, lift my body up and then swing both feet backwards onto the step. I would then put weight on my right leg and move my hands up the railing for the next lift and swing. I felt clever climbing the stairs that way. It was much less painful than walking with the crutches. Once at the top, I awkwardly turned around and started my routine of placing the crutch tips forward, raising up on the toes of my right foot and then letting my left leg swing forward. I eventually made it to our guest bedroom and was able, with Linda's help, to get up onto the bed and lie down. I was exhausted from the effort and intense pain. Eventually the pain eased and Linda, seeing that I was safe on the bed, told me to rest while she went to the grocery store.

For years I had volunteered and helped injured high school varsity football and Lacrosse athletes off the field and treated their injuries. This was just another on-field injury. I could figure this out. While Linda was gone, I decided to try and get an idea of what was injured and how serious it was. I couldn't drag my left heel up the bed to flex the hip, so I grabbed my thigh with both hands and used my arms to pull the leg up. I got my hip to a 90-degree bend and then gripping my thigh tightly I moved it around in small circles to check out my hip joint. I had no hip pain. Next, with my feet on the bed and both hips and knees bent, I resisted pushing my knees apart and it was not painful, so I resisted pushing my knees together which caused left groin pain. Maybe it really was a severe groin strain. I also wondered if I had knocked my pelvis out of alignment when I hit the ground which could cause similar symptoms of buttocks and groin pain. I don't know how I managed, but for those of you who enjoy Yoga, you are familiar with the pigeon pose. I got down on the floor, which was a significant feat, and got into the pigeon pose with my right leg crossed under my stomach and my left leg and hip extended back. I didn't feel much pain. I then switched so that my left leg was crossed under my stomach. Bad idea.

"Good judgement comes from experience; experience comes from bad judgement." [3]

Somewhere during this self-evaluation, I decided it might be a good idea to go to the emergency room. When Linda got home, I began the lengthy process of making my way back through the house to the garage, down the stairs and into the vehicle using my now tried-and-true method of walking. Once I was in the vehicle, Linda drove us to the emergency room.

Emergency Room

After being admitted to the emergency room, the doctor determined, based on my symptoms, to order a CT scan. I thought I had experienced pain after the fall and while making my way up the stairs and into the bedroom and then back down the stairs and into the vehicle for the drive to the emergency room. I was wrong. Transferring from the soft bed onto the rigid plastic backboard, lying on the rigid plastic backboard during the CT scan, then transferring back on the bed was excruciating. Luckily, as I lay there in bed, while waiting for the results of the CT scan, the pain started to ease. Eventually, the emergency room doctor, whom I knew, told us that I had two displaced fractures: one in the superior left pubic rami and one in the inferior left pubic rami as well as a gapped sacroiliac joint and sacral fracture on the right. I wouldn't be going home.

We talked about surgery, and he told us there were two traumatology specialists at the hospital. I knew one of them because I had treated many of his patients and he had also operated on some family members. I was not familiar with the other surgeon. We were told he was a good surgeon but didn't have much of a bedside manner. This surgeon would be able to operate on me on Monday whereas the other wouldn't be able to operate on me until Tuesday. I chose the first surgeon thinking that I would have the surgery on Monday and then take off one week of work and then return to work with the idea that I would be able to sit on a stool and treat patients.

View out the window of my room.

Again, either an optimist or someone in complete denial. Either way, it turned out to be a pipe dream. After receiving the news that I wouldn't be going home they transferred us to a hospital room. I was placed on complete bedrest. The irony of the room they put me in was that I could look out the window and see the emergency room drive up entrance with Trauma Center in bold letters above the entrance to the emergency room.

Journal Entry May 23, 2021

Laying around in bed makes me crazy but at least the pain is not severe. I feel an achiness in the right buttocks but not much in the left groin if I lay still. To drag my left heel up the bed to bend my knee requires use of both my hands but it really hurts in the groin, so I try not to do it much. I can't roll to either side without a lot of pain, so I just stay flat on my back. I use the hand-held urinal rather than get up to use the bathroom. Our son, Nick stopped by and gave me a priesthood blessing. I was not in pain just lying around in bed all day, but I was in need of comfort given my new life reality. I was able to feel the peace that accompanied the priesthood blessing. What a great privilege to receive one from our son.

Journal Entry May 24, 2021

I lay in bed from Saturday afternoon until early this morning. I was wheeled down to the pre-op area and put into a curtained cubicle to wait to speak with the doctor, whom we hadn't yet met. When he came in, he looked at me and said, "Oh, you're the wrong person. They must have moved you up on the schedule." That was not a comforting start to our relationship. He then pulled up the CT scan images on his computer, studied them for a few minutes, and told us that if all I had were the two left pubic rami fractures, he wouldn't operate and conversely, if all I had was the right sacral fracture he wouldn't operate but because I had the three fractures and the right sacroiliac joint was spread, the pelvis was less stable. His plan was to fix the right sacral fracture and let the two left pubic rami fractures heal on their own. Linda then asked if he would have the surgery if it were him, to which he replied, "I don't know. I have never had these fractures." He told us he would use screws to stabilize the sacral fracture and that I would be twelve to fourteen weeks non-weight bearing on both legs.

Twelve to fourteen weeks! Are you kidding me? I was so shocked I couldn't say anything. Linda looked at me and knew I was struggling mentally with the news. *How could I be non-weight bearing for that long? How could I not work for that long? How would we survive financially? I don't know if it was shock or sudden depression or fear, but I was in a very dark place mentally and shut down. So much for my plan to have the surgery and then go back to work in one week even if I could only work on patients while seated.*

And now, I, Moroni, would speak somewhat concerning these things; I would show unto the world that faith is things which are hoped for and not seen; wherefore, dispute not because ye see not, for ye receive no witness until after the trial of your faith. (Ether 12:6)

Looking Back

Just for a minute, let me backtrack and share some history that will give you a better understanding of why the surgeon's statement of being laid up for twelve to fourteen weeks shocked me so badly. In July of 2019, my friend Noel Hyde, was leading a long line of 16 to18 year-old young women up a single-track trail at an LDS church girl's camp located in the mountains east of Heber City, Utah. They all carried back packs so that they could camp overnight on the mountain. I was bringing up the rear to help out if any of the young women had any problems. I came up over a small rise and a girl was sitting on a log having difficulty. She was tired, anxious and short of breath. I talked to her and after a few minutes she was more calm so we decided to continue hiking with me carrying her pack and letting her hike at a slower pace until she felt better. At one point I had her sit down on the ground at the side of the trail. I looked behind us and then when I turned back to her, she had fainted. Someone radioed the camp missionaries down below and they sent a side by side up to transport the young lady off the mountain. I sat in the bed of the vehicle with my arm around the outside of the roll bar to stabilize her head if she fainted. The trail was narrow and rough and at one point while trying to maneuver between two trees on an angled slope the vehicle tipped on its side, and I was thrown out and injured my shoulder. Two months later, at the end of September 2019, I had two large rotator cuff tears, and a biceps tendon repaired.

In January 2020, while the shoulder was still healing, I started experiencing significant low back, right buttocks, and leg pain. It got to the point where I had to kneel by the exercise equipment in the gym, while patients performed their exercises. I could only walk about fifty feet before I would have to lean on something because of the severity of the right leg pain. There were some mornings when I got up early to get ready for work that I chose to crawl initially because the pain was so intense. I tried to exercise and calm down the pain as I had many times over the years but this time it was not meant to be. On Friday, February 28, 2020, I had an MRI of my back. On Saturday, the 29th my friend, Dr. Shepherd, reviewed the MRI and read the report. On Monday March 2nd after Dr. Shepherd described my symptoms and showed the MRI to Dr. Smith, a neurosurgeon, Dr. Smith scheduled me for surgery on March 5th, before he had even seen or talked with me. When I met with him, we reviewed the MRI and after listening to his recommendations, I agreed to the surgery. I underwent a discectomy at L3-4 on March 5, 2020.

Recovery

I was making great progress with the rotator cuff repair and the back was healing nicely. Just when I was ready to start seeing patients, at the beginning of April, the Covid 19 pandemic started and the Ogden Athletic Club, where my clinic is located, closed for two and a half months. They permitted us to keep the clinic open, but the problem was even though I felt ready to treat patients again, there were very few patients to be seen. Sometimes we only had 1-2 patients a day for two physical therapists.

Then, in August of 2020, I was involved in a car collision. I was taken by ambulance to the emergency room. I sustained a cervical whiplash, and a broken rib. I was relieved that my low back seemed to be fine. I was back at work before lunch. I struggled through each day treating patients with a broken rib. A week after the accident, I had a setback with my low back and right leg pain. One week later, to my relief the back and leg pain resolved. Once the rib was healed, I was able to gradually work back into a vigorous exercise program.

I recovered from both surgeries and the car accident and in February of 2021, I wrote in my journal that I was skinning up (hiking uphill on special snow skis with skins on the bottom to give you traction) from the main lodge at Snow Basin Ski resort, two miles uphill to the top of the gondola faster in 2021 than I had two winters before, before either the shoulder or back injuries and surgeries, and the car accident. I was so happy to be back in shape again. I got back to exercising, working, doing gardening and yard work, riding horses and other projects. I felt like I was healthy, and I felt much younger than my 64 years of age.

You can now understand a little better why I was so devastated when the surgeon told me I would be laid up for twelve to fourteen weeks. I had worked so hard to get back in shape and get my health back and now, I was faced with something far worse than the three previous injuries and the two surgeries combined.

Notes

1 Young John Taylor, Paul Thomas Smith, Ibid., p. 266.
2 Faith Is Not Blind, Bruce C. Hafen and Marie K. Hafen, quote Elder Neal A. Maxwell, p. 58-59
3 This aphorism was attributed to Dr Kerr L White

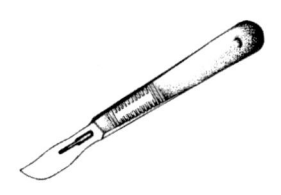

3

Surgery

"Think it not strange concerning the fiery trial, which is to try you, as though some strange thing happened to you." (1 Peter 4:12)

I don't remember much after the surgeon told me how long I would be non-weight bearing. My mind was in a deep, dark maze of disbelief. The next thing I knew, they were wheeling me over to the operating room. I was in mental shock. The anesthesiologist assigned to my case recognized me. I had treated him and members of his family in my physical therapy clinic over several years. He started talking about a mutual friend of ours, John Schlichte, who owns the Warrior Rizen Ranch that is dedicated to serving families that have either lost a family member or had one injured during military or police service. As we talked, he wheeled me down the long, sterile, and semi-empty hallways. The conversation helped take my mind off the surgery and I was able to laugh and relax a little.

When I woke up after the surgery, Linda told me that the surgeon had told her that I would be non-weight bearing for a minimum of six weeks on both legs. I was surprised but at least I didn't feel quite as bad. Still, six weeks in bed seemed so long, especially for someone that thought of sleeping in as staying in bed until 6 a.m. Later that evening, after situating us in a room on the rehab floor, our nurse came in, introduced herself and then walked over to the whiteboard on the wall and wrote her name, the name of the CNA, the date, my name and then wrote that I would be non-weight bearing on my right leg and weight bearing as tolerated on my left leg. Linda and I were caught off guard. We looked at each other in shock and then Linda told her what she had been told by the surgeon and asked her to check the surgeon's orders. The nurse checked the orders and then showed us the post op report and orders. She had been correct with what she had written on the whiteboard. We were incredibly surprised because after surgery he had written one set of orders and told Linda something entirely different. I was thrilled to hear the news. Then a question came to mind: Before the surgery I could bear weight on my right leg but couldn't tolerate any weight on my left leg. How was I supposed to put weight on my left leg, with two unrepaired pelvic fractures and not on my right leg? Another mental conflict. On the one hand I was excited with the surgeon's post-op orders but on the other hand I didn't think it was possible that I would be able to walk and bear weight on my left leg.

Rehab Unit Hospital

The first night, as I lay in bed in my hospital room, the negative thoughts were like runaway cattle, stampeding through my mind. I really felt dark mentally and emotionally thinking of the cost of the surgery and ongoing charges for care including being hospitalized. The realization that I wouldn't be able to work for some time along with the thought that I couldn't go home because I wouldn't be able to get up the stairs using my left leg, hit hard. I was all alone with these dark thoughts, and it was not a great place to be.

First Miracles

As I lay in bed that first night, I was extremely uncomfortable lying there with my legs out straight so, despite the pain of trying to drag my heel up to bend my leg, I decided to do it to make lying in bed more tolerable. Prior to the surgery, I had to use both arms to pull my left leg up and had to do it slowly because of pain but this time I was able to drag my heel up and down the bed three times without using my arms. How was that possible?

The surgeon hadn't fixed the two fractures on the left. I was thrilled and I found myself praying and thanking my Heavenly Father for that gift. Here was my first miracle.

I have found throughout my life that when you are going through tough times, you have highs and lows, things you look forward to and things you dread. Over the next few days, there were both. There were even some humorous moments. Linda brought a book to the hospital and would read it to me. The title of the book was Lost Apothecary.

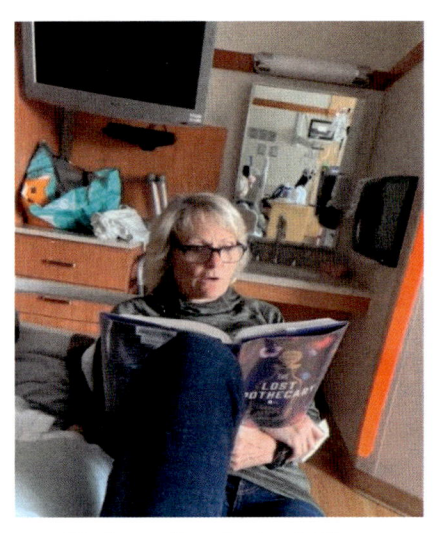

It was a story of women that were being abused, mistreated, or cheated on that would go to a certain Apothecary after hours and were taken into a private back room. Here they were given various powders or mixtures to administer to their husbands that would gradually poison them to death. The irony was not lost on me and whenever I commented about it, Linda would let out an evil laugh.

Linda reading the book "Lost Apothecary"

I came to dread bedding changes. They would have me roll onto one side and push the old bedding underneath my back to the middle of the bed, then put the new bedding on that side and put the rest of it up against the rolled up dirty bedding tucked up against the middle of my back and then as they rolled me onto the other side, they would pull out the old bedding and pull the other half of the new bedding out from under me and fit it to the mattress. It is a technique I helped with when I used to work in the University of Utah hospital and in nursing homes. The problem for me was that anytime I had to roll onto my left side, it put pressure directly on the two unhealed fractures and the pain was very intense.

About four days after surgery, while going through a bedding change, I started to roll with the help of a nurse, and I was able to roll onto my left side with just moderate pain. I was so surprised, but it put a smile on my face. I offered another prayer of gratitude. God hadn't forgotten me. Another miracle, not like the parting of the Red Sea, and yet for me it was just as amazing.

As I pondered that first night, then remembered the back-to-back miracles, my faith seemed to increase and comfort came to my heart. I now had hope that I would be able to stand on my left leg. As I lay in bed later that night, all alone in my hospital room, I had hope for more miracles. I didn't know if the miracle would be me being able to tolerate weight bearing on my left leg, allowing me to walk a little, or a miraculous healing of the left pelvic fractures or if it would be relief of the excruciating left pelvic pain, allowing me to be more comfortable throughout the healing process. I felt like Heavenly Father was aware of my struggles and was blessing me.

4
Storm After the Calm

"Life is what happens while you're making other plans." [1]

    I was excited to be walking, supporting my weight on crutches and my left leg which four days before couldn't tolerate any weight. A few days after I started walking, I started experiencing intense pain at times, not while walking but when sitting in the wheelchair. There were times I could hardly tolerate sitting in the wheelchair even with a special seat cushion. Then one day, as I tried to sit partway up in bed, I lost control of my bladder and wet the bed. It happened again a little later. Then I noticed that I lost the muscle strength in the pelvic floor muscles so now I had problems with bowel movements. The severe pain I would feel while sitting and occasionally while walking continued to be intermittent but became more intense. The doctor on the rehab floor would tell me I was doing too much. He would check my lower leg muscles for strength, ask if I could feel my toes and then walk out of the room. It was like he had already decided that these symptoms were due to me being up too much and dismissed the possibility that there might be something more serious. Hmm, pelvic surgery followed by loss of bowel and bladder control. It seemed like a red flag to me. I kept silent despite my growing concerns.

Journal Entry 5/27/2021

*   Yesterday started great but then it went south. They transferred me from the postop unit to the inpatient rehab unit. I have been lying*

in bed from when I walked at 1 o'clock the day before until 2:30 today. Then they got me up and had me walk farther than yesterday, probably one hundred feet. I started having pain across my sacral area that was so intense that tilting the bed up to eat my meals was impossible. The pain became very severe in just a couple of minutes and because I couldn't sit up, I didn't eat most of my dinner and no one was there to help me because it was late at night. The pain continued and made it almost intolerable to raise the head of the bed up just long enough to use the urinal. I talked to the nurse about my concerns. I told her that I couldn't even sit up in bed so how could I do anything else that I needed to do and then asked her to call the doctor. That was at about 8:00 p.m. A little after 10 p.m., a new nurse came in and I asked what the doctor said about my pain. She looked at me with a puzzled look on her face and told me that no one had called the doctor. I was really discouraged and frustrated. Wasn't anybody listening to me? Was anyone documenting these problems in my chart notes? She called the doctor and eventually they gave me some medicine.

Journal Entry May 28, 2021

Today started off very rough. When I sat up in the bed, I had severe burning pain down the back of my left thigh and into my groin. I had slept well through the night, so I was not sure why. I got up to walk with a therapist and the burning pain just intensified it, so I sat down in the wheelchair. I then started to feel like I was going into shock, I felt lightheaded, and I was sweating. The therapist wheeled me down to the physical therapy gym, and I went up and down a set of four or five steps a couple times and then I felt like I was going into shock again and so I lay down on their hard mat. They put ice on me, and the queasiness and the cold sweats left. We did a few exercises, which was fine but then when we had to sit me up it was to the left side with the unhealed fractures that weren't repaired, and I don't usually sit up on that side and I had intense pain. It was all I could do *to get up into the wheelchair. They helped me transfer back into bed and eventually the pain subsided but in the meantime the doctor had ordered x-rays and new medication. During occupational therapy, we were sitting in a padded wheelchair out in the hallway near a window. I was having intense groin and buttocks pain. Just when I was ready to ask them to take me back to my room so that I could lie down and relieve the pain they said they were ready for me down in the x-ray department. They took me down in the wheelchair. By the time I arrived I was perspiring from holding myself up with my arms, and I was in significant pain. They said I could either stand or lie down on the hard table for the x-ray and I chose to stand. The thought of rolling onto that hard x-ray table didn't sound good to me. They did all the x-rays, and I sat back down in the wheelchair. To my surprise and relief, the pain was half of what it was before I stood up for the x-rays. It didn't make sense as I thought about it, but I was truly grateful for any relief from the pain. Another little blessing. By the time we got back to Linda, I was almost falling asleep and because the pain was so minimal, we were able to go outside in the sunshine. It felt so good to be outside in the fresh air. When we got back to my room, I was able to get back into bed with almost no pain and take a little nap before the physical therapist came to take me down for another session.*

Chastening

The doctor had watched the episode of me becoming lightheaded earlier in the day as he sat at the nurse's station making phone calls. After my afternoon therapy session, as I walked past the desk with the physical therapist, the doctor looked up and when he saw me, he set the phone down and in no uncertain terms told me that I was doing too much. He told me that I had pelvic fractures, and pelvic fractures were very painful, and I needed to slow down and be more patient. Linda, believing him, became emotional and walked back to the room.

I wanted to yell out, "I am not over doing it. Something isn't right!" But I didn't. I couldn't understand why I could walk sometimes without pain and occasionally sit in the wheelchair with only moderate pain and yet other times I had to lie down in bed to stop the unbearable pain. I eventually gave in and decided they must be right. I still had two pelvic fractures on the weight bearing side that hadn't been repaired. I walked back to the room, got into bed and once the pain subsided, Linda and I had an emotional heart-to-heart talk. I promised her I would slow down. It didn't matter because from that time on the storm intensified and the pain occurred more frequently.

The pain was always in the forefront of my mind, but it was not the only concern at this time. I was still having bowel and bladder issues. I had to look down to see if I was finished, and if I didn't, I would sometimes have an accident on the bathroom floor as I stood up, thinking I was finished. I was also having problems with bowel movements due to muscle weakness. I had reported the issues many times to the nurses and just assumed the surgeon would be informed and stop by to check up on me. He never visited me after the surgery. Maybe he was never told about my issues.

It was at this time that I started wondering if the surgeon had inadvertently put a screw into a nerve. I spoke with a friend of mine, who is also a medical doctor, at length about it. We decided that if a screw were hitting a nerve that I would have had excruciating pain as soon as I woke up from surgery and it would have been constant. As it was, within 4-5 minutes of lying down in bed, the pain, no matter how intense, usually subsided. So, I continued to limit my activity as promised. I continued to work with the physical and occupational therapists, but I decided how far I would walk and how much I would do. My son Chris, who is a nurse practitioner, kept telling Linda to warn me not to try and progress too quickly because if I did, even if I were in excruciating pain, they would discharge me because pain alone was not a reason to keep me in the hospital.

After the doctor told us I was doing too much, and I had promised Linda I would stop pushing myself, I told the therapists that I wouldn't do the stairs until just before I was discharged. I knew I had the arm strength to get up the stairs and I wanted to let my pelvis heal more. I also continued to limit my walking to much shorter distances.

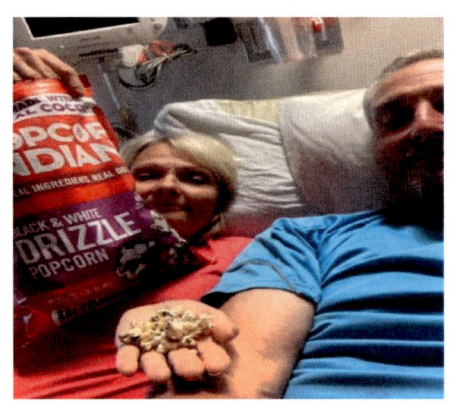

Popcorn and movie night in the hospital bed

The day before I was to be discharged from the hospital, I had several tests to pass before the therapists could sign off on my abilities to go home. They had me walk back and forth across an 8 foot long, 2 inch thick soft foam mat several times, which, had I really thought about it I would have refused because I wasn't going to be walking on grass or dirt trails so it was a pointless exercise that was putting unnecessary stress on my pelvis, but I was in full "I am going to pass these tests and go home" mode. Nothing was going to keep me in the hospital. I was tired of nights away from Linda, of being awakened throughout the night and all the busyness of the hospital, even in the middle of the night. After the foam mats came the stair test. The stairs in the therapy room only had four steps so I went up and down them three times. I had no problem. I would be able to manage the stairs at home. The occupational therapists were waiting for me when I finished with the physical therapists. They wheeled me down to a room with a toilet, shower and bath and had me transfer from the wheelchair to a bath bench, then swing my legs over the edge of the tub by myself to see if I could take care of bathroom and bathing needs safely. I passed all their tests but by the time I got back to my room, I was an 8/10 on the pain scale. When I got back to my room, I needed to go to the bathroom. Earlier, when Linda and I had talked about going home, she had told me that if she was taking me home that I needed to be able to walk to the bathroom and not use the portable urinal. Up to this point in time I had used the portable urinal most of the time rather than walk into the bathroom in my room at the hospital. Although I was in a lot of pain from a couple of hours of tests, I decided I would walk into the bathroom to keep my promise. I did it and then made it back to bed where I waited for the storm of pain to subside.

The next morning, I was discharged to home. The drive home was very painful and fatiguing because I was trying to hold my bottom up off the car seat for the 20-minute drive home using the console and armrest. Every time we turned a corner, went through a dip, or hit a pothole in the road the pain intensified. After arriving home, I was able to go up the twelve steps into the house without much difficulty and walk back to the guest bedroom where I was able to lie down on the bed, exhausted. That day I got up and walked into the bathroom four times, twenty feet to the bathroom and then twenty painful feet back to bed. That was double what I had been doing at the hospital after I had started self-limiting my activity. The walk to the bathroom was usually okay but sitting on the toilet was torture and then once the pain kicked in, I had a tough time walking back to bed. I keep using the term walk. My walk was to place both crutches out in front of me and then swing both legs forward.

The morning after I was discharged, I woke up and I needed to go to the bathroom. I started to push up onto my elbows so that I could swing my legs off the side of the bed, but I was hit with a wave of pain so intense that I had to lie back down. I could hardly move, couldn't sit up, I couldn't even get up onto my elbows. I was literally only able to lie there in bed. I couldn't overcome the pain. When Linda came in after waking up, I was in bad shape. I told her I didn't think I could take the pain I was feeling much longer and that if it kept up, I would be calling an ambulance to take me to the hospital. It was then that I remembered that I had finished my daily dose of Prednisone about 48 hours earlier. Before being discharged from the hospital they had given me a Medrol dose pack for use at home that I hadn't started yet. It was a tapered dose, so I was to take four pills, then three pills and then two pills each for a prescribed number of days eventually tapering down to one pill a day until the pills were gone. I took the first four pill dose and waited. It worked miraculously. About six hours after the first dose, I could sit up and walk to the bathroom with almost no pain.

Journal Entry June 8, 2021 Reality moment

The sacral nerves are somewhat damaged or inflamed but whatever the case is it affects my bowel and bladder. This morning, I got up on my walker and felt like I needed to have a bowel movement. I tried to bear down a little bit to see if I did and I wet myself because I couldn't control my bladder. I hope the nerves come back or I will be wearing adult diapers. Ha.

First Surgery Follow Up Appointment

On June 9th, I was scheduled to have a follow up appointment with the surgeon. I was very concerned about the drive to and from the hospital and sitting at the doctor's office. Although the Prednisone was helpful, sitting was something I tried to avoid. I still couldn't sit up in bed. If I put two pillows behind me, I could tolerate a semi-reclined position for about 10 minutes. One of our good friends, Diane, had brought over a wheelchair for me to use while at home. I remember one day some friends came over. I had just transferred into the wheelchair and thought it would be nice if Linda pushed me out onto the back balcony where we could visit with them. It took about two minutes to push me out to the balcony and by the time we got there, I was supporting all my weight with my arms, was shaking, and perspiring with the overwhelming pain. I couldn't handle it. I was embarrassed but I had to immediately have Linda push me back to the room where it was all I could do to transfer back into bed.

Prior to the day of my doctor's appointment, I had called his office and spoken with someone at the front desk. I told her of my concerns about the drive and sitting during my appointment. I asked if he could do a virtual appointment over the internet, and she informed me that that wouldn't be possible. I then asked if when I arrived, I could go back to the exam room and lie down until the doctor was ready to see me. She said they would do their best to accommodate me.

June 9th arrived and although anxious about the drive to and from the hospital and sitting in a wheelchair while waiting for the doctor, I put my faith in the Lord. I woke up much earlier than usual. I had real concerns. I pondered, prayed, and read from the scriptures early that morning while Linda slept, and then I determined I would trust in the Lord and put my faith to the test.

Linda helped get me situated in the car and we were off to the hospital. I was tired by the time we arrived at the hospital, having tried to hold my bottom up off the seat as best I could for 20 minutes or so. Once there, a volunteer brought out a wheelchair, steadied it as I transferred from my crutches into the chair and then pushed me up to the doctor's office on the second floor. The receptionist at the front desk was very sympathetic and after I completed the required paperwork, called another staff member to roll me back into an exam room where I was able to lie down on an exam table. I was so thankful because we had a long wait before seeing the doctor.

I was lying on the exam table which was up against the wall with my left side to the wall. The doctor came in and we talked for some time. He asked me where I was experiencing the most pain and I replied on the left side and pointed where the pain was on my right pelvis since the left side was against the wall. He made a point of telling me I was pointing to the right side while talking about pain on the left side. I explained that because my left side was against the wall it was easier to use the right side to show where the left side hurt. My second time talking to this surgeon and the second bad start to a conversation. I now realized the rumors about his bedside manner were true.

The next part of our conversation was confusing to me. After describing my issues with loss of control of bladder and bowel function, he looked at me and said, "That doesn't make sense. Things like that happen to old men." I had been telling the hospital staff about these symptoms the entire time I was in the hospital. I had told the nurses, and the rehab doctor. I then asked him if the nurses or rehab doctor had informed him of the pain and problems I had been having since the surgery. He mumbled something but it was rather vague. He then asked about a prostate procedure I had had a few years before and asked if that was the problem, to which I replied. "No." I told him I was not having any of these problems until a few days after the surgery. Eventually, after asking more questions, he told me he was going to order a CT scan stat and that he would let me know the result within 1-2 hours. Unfortunately, the hospital radiology schedule was full, so he ordered it at the off-campus building, requiring me to sit in the wheelchair as they wheeled me out to our vehicle, get back into the vehicle, drive over to the other building, transfer into another wheelchair and get pushed into the radiology department for the CT scan and then have an even longer drive home.

After the CT scan, we drove over to the Stonehenge Care Center where I had been approved to stay. We parked outside but we felt unsettled and didn't go inside. We decided we should wait and hear what the CT scan showed before being admitted into the care center and drove home. Shortly afterwards, the doctor called and told us that one of the screws was in a bad place and he wanted to remove it the next morning. We called the care center, explained the situation and they agreed to put the admission on hold. It was interesting that I had worked so hard to get admitted to the care center and then when it was approved, I had felt uncomfortable. Now I knew why.

I spent a restless night, waking up early in the middle of the night thinking about all that had transpired the day before. When Linda woke up, it was about 5 a.m. We were supposed to be at the hospital by 6 a.m. On the drive over to the hospital we talked about the care center. I decided that after the surgery I would be fine returning home. Here I was again, either an optimist or in complete denial or as Linda would say I was being "tupid" not "smrt."

We arrived at the hospital, had a volunteer bring out a wheelchair and then take us up to the pre-op waiting area. I was in a lot of pain from the drive over and I asked the lady working at the registration desk if I could go back and lie down somewhere while waiting to be taken back for the surgery and was told there was no place for me to lie down. By the time they wheeled me back I was in so much pain that I was shaking and perspiring and was not in a great mood. The other people in the waiting room were looking at me like something was wrong with me but I couldn't help it. The pain was starting to overwhelm me, and I was really upset that the lady was ignoring my request to find someplace where I could lie down like they had for my doctor's appointment. When the nurse came out to wheel me back, she asked me if I could stand up to be weighed. I didn't cuss but I felt like it as I did my version of popping up out of the wheelchair, to stand up and relieve the excruciating pressure I felt while seated in the chair.

Eventually I was wheeled down to a pre-op cubicle. The first person to come in to talk to us was the surgeon's physician assistant. He told us that the surgeon had been nervous the night before after having seen where the screw had been placed and that he had consulted with a neurosurgeon about how best to proceed and was told to back the screw out very slowly. The surgery apparently went well and when I woke up, I had very little pain.

Once I was fully awake, Linda and I started discussing our options. The surgeon assumed I would go home after the surgery. I was in favor of going home. We discussed our options with a nurse, the physician assistant, the case worker and finally spoke with our home ward bishop, Bishop Stucki. He was very familiar with how insurance companies work and gave us some wise advice.

He explained that if I went home and had problems, I would likely not be able to be admitted to the care center. If I went to the care center and had problems I would be in a good place and if I progressed quickly, I could have a shorter stay at the care center and then go home. Linda and I agreed that it made sense and we discussed the option of going to the care center instead of home with the nurse, physician assistant, a physical therapist, and the case manager and all agreed it was the prudent thing to do. It was early evening by this time and the case manager was not sure she could get approval to transfer over to the care center in time. We prayed it would work out and a short while later she came back in with a smile and a somewhat surprised expression on her face as she explained that she had never received approval that quickly in her career. Our prayers had been answered. Another miracle.

The last concern was the drive to the care center. They said they would transport me in a wheelchair in a van to the care center. There was no way I was going to agree to that after the pain I had experienced that morning on the drive to the hospital. I told them I would have Linda drive me over in our vehicle and that way I could lie down on the back seat. They were not excited about that idea, but there was no way I was going to ride over in a wheelchair.

Nothing more was said until the van arrived to transport me. There was not much room in the recovery room, so they wheeled me out into the hallway and to my dismay and relief they had a gurney to transport me to the care center. Another prayer answered. Another miracle.

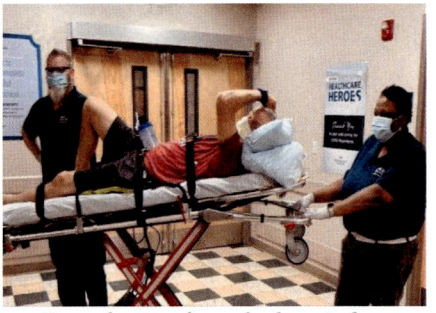

Transferring from the hospital to Stonehenge Care Center

They rolled me out to the front of the hospital and then up a ramp into the van. The van had a sunken floor so I was below window level. I had the strangest feeling that this is what it would be like if you were being transported in a hearse. I shared my thought with the driver and his assistant and we all had a good laugh. Once at the care center, they transferred me onto a bed. It was a basic rigid plastic mattress without any padding. It was supposed to have an air mattress topper on it, but no one had put one on the mattress. I lay on the hard mattress from 7:30 until 11:45 p.m. I was tired and uncomfortable. It had been a long day, and this was not the ending I had envisioned. Eventually they brought in the air mattress. They set it on the firm-dynamic setting and then left the room. The air mattress was divided into four-inch sections. As the cycle progressed, a four-inch section would inflate until very firm and then after a few seconds would deflate a little and then the next section would inflate. As each section inflated the pressure on my pelvis and lower back was uncomfortable. I started thinking I won't be able to tolerate this bed. What have I done? I made a mistake coming here. How am I going to survive if I can't sit up and can't tolerate this mattress? I should have gone home. About 3:15 in the morning a CNA came in and I told her how uncomfortable I was, so she changed the air mattress setting to the soft-static setting and I soon was able to relax and fall asleep for a few hours. From then on it was going to be great I hoped.

Journal Entry 6/12/2021

Rough night last night with achiness in sacrum that wouldn't let up. Got to sleep about 5 a.m. No changes in bladder function today. They gave me a super bowel cleaner last night and I messed my shorts a little getting to the bathroom and then got diarrhea and have made eleven more trips to the bathroom. My best guess is about 580' of walking. It is hard to hurry walking with a broken pelvis and knowing if the bowel movement starts while walking you can't stop it, and you will make a mess. That is more walking than I have done since the accident. Skipping breakfast didn't help. I was very shaky.

I have started feeling impatient to have the nerves healed again, wanting that miracle on my time, and had to repent and turn it back to Heavenly Father and His timeline. Then while reading in the scriptures, I came across this verse:" Yea, and how is it that ye have forgotten that the Lord is able to do all things according to his will, for the children of men, if it so be that they exercise faith in him? Wherefore, let us be faithful to him." (1 Nephi 7:12)

Journal Entry 6/17/2021

"A university student told his elders quorum this story:

He was raised on a farm. Shortly after he was ordained a deacon, they had a pregnant cow, and his parents said that he could have the calf to raise as his own. This would be his first. One day, while his parents were gone, the cow went into premature labor and the calf was born. Then suddenly the cow began to roll all over the calf, and he realized she was trying to kill it. He cried out to the Lord for help. Not thinking about how much more the cow weighed than he did, he pushed on her with all his strength and somehow moved her away. He picked up the lifeless – looking calf in his arms and looked at it, the tears running down his cheeks. Then he remembered that he had every right to ask for the Lord's help. So, he prayed again from the depths of his boyish, believing heart. Before long, the little animal began to move and breathe normally. He knew his prayer had been heard.

Then the tears welled up in his eyes and he said, "Brethren, I tell you that story because I do not think I would do now what I did then. Now that I am older and less naïve, I know better than to expect the Lords help in a situation like that. If I relived that experience now, I would probably believe it was a coincidence. I am not sure how I've changed, but I may have lost something valuable. He felt less childlike, less believing." [2]

Journal Entry 6/19/2021

Last night, we celebrated our 39th wedding anniversary by drinking sparkling apple juice, eating buttered popcorn, Cheetos and watching two movies. My sister, Peggy, and her husband Cody bought all of it plus a card for Linda. It was a low-key celebration but very relaxing.

I had a nice, long quiet period this morning to pray. I had a lot to talk about with Heavenly Father and covered a lot of topics. I had a lot of things to thank Him for, more than I deserve but for which I am grateful. Following my prayers I read in the Book of Mormon, then the book, Led by Divine Design. A scripture reference from that book stood out in my mind: Counsel with the Lord in all thy doings, and he will direct thee for good; yea, when thou liest down at night lie down unto the Lord, that he may watch over you in your sleep; and when thou risest in the morning let thy heart be full of thanks unto God; (Alma 37:37)

It is usually very quiet between 5:00 and 6:00 a.m. so it is a good time to pray and read scriptures and other religious books. Anyway, it is nice, and it is usually the time when I get important insights. A few hours later I turned on the TV and I don't know what triggered my emotions but suddenly I found myself staring out the window feeling lonely or something like that and I was emotional. My life has been completely turned upside down by the injury and the added insult of bowel and bladder dysfunction caused by the misplaced screw that compressed the sacral nerves. I am going to be in trouble financially, don't know what the future of this nerve damage will be, the mental and emotional as well as physical stress have been tremendous, and I am in a position where pushing myself harder is detrimental.

I am so dependent on Heavenly Father to help me get through this trial and learn what I need to learn. I have had some very dark *and tough times, especially when I was experiencing the severe pain caused by the screw pushing on the sacral nerves. There were times when it was so severe that I pled to get out of the chair to lie down and stop the pain. I have had sciatic nerve pain many times, but never have I experienced pain like this.*

Journal Entry 6/21/2021

Had a better night. Forgot to take the anti-inflammatory medication but other than waking a few times to go to the bathroom I slept/dozed from midnight until about 5:30 which was nice. I am ready to do therapy a couple of times today as over the weekend there was no therapy.

Concerns on my mind this week are getting the hospital to create a contract covering costs from the surgeon's mistake in surgery and future costs related to bowel and bladder dysfunction from the nerve damage, and the follow up visit with the surgeon. I am hoping he will order 2 more weeks in the care facility because Linda is flying to Oregon on Thursday and if I am discharged to home, I'll be alone, and she will be gone for 8 days.

I had my morning prayer, read from the Book of Mormon and two other books by general authorities and then had time to just lay back and have some quiet time to think. No great revelations or answers but it was very peaceful. My goal is to continue to set aside quiet time once I am back to a more normal life. For years I have worked out in the gym and then gone into my office and read scriptures in the quiet of the early morning. Then, after reading scriptures and praying I have listened to a general conference talk. It has been a nice routine. Now it is a necessary routine to help me get through this trial.

Therapy went well. Had one urination issue today but otherwise it was okay. I have to look to make sure I am done urinating when using the urinal or on the toilet or I leak in bed or on the floor.

Journal Entry 6/25/2021

    Last night I got down almost on my hands and knees as I was so desperate for help. I had to hang on the bed with my arms and support most of my weight on my chest, but it didn't hurt. I don't know why but I wanted to kneel to pray. I sat up in the wheelchair and ate dinner for the first time since my injury on May 22nd. That was a big event. Then I wheeled out to the back door in my wheelchair and looked outside for a few minutes. I wheeled back into the room then walked down the hall and back about as far as I do with the therapists. When I got back to the room, I sat in the recliner for 20 minutes or so.

    Fairly good progress. Still feeling restless and lonely. I didn't realize how important it was to have a variety of good books to read. Without them I feel like I am going to lose my mind. I sat in the wheelchair again for 15 minutes or more. I was talking to the nurse. Then, I started to perspire sitting there. I wonder if it was a little shock because of discomfort and how long I sat there.

Journal Entry 6/26/2021

    I was able to work hard in therapy in the morning and afternoon. I worked up a sweat. I was able to walk farther than I have been without pain in the leg just fatigue in the arms since they are holding a lot of my weight still. I tried two different things that I haven't been able to do. I lay on my left side for about two minutes and then turned over and lay on my right side for about two minutes. I had a little achiness but no significant pain. Later, I rolled over on my stomach on the mattress, and I was able to lie there without pain. I was not so concerned about lying on my stomach as I was about rolling over on the pelvis and maybe injuring something, but it was just fine.

Journal Entry 6/27/2021

    Woke up and after prayer and reading scriptures, I started preparing for a virtual bishopric meeting by looking at the agenda he *sent me and the names he was considering for various positions. I tried to ponder and think and get inspiration on who would be good in which positions. It was enjoyable being part of the bishopric meeting. I was of some assistance in sharing some of my thoughts and feelings. I also joined the ward council meeting for a little bit. I then turned on my computer to watch my home ward sacrament meeting over zoom. Just before that I happened to see an email from my employer. They were letting me know my health insurance was being cut off as of May 31st and that if I wanted to continue to have insurance, I could go on cobra insurance which basically means I pay the entire amount. No income and now a huge increase in my insurance premium. Why did they wait a month to let me know? What about all the medical care I have received since May 31st. I was stressed out.*

Journal Entry 6/28/2021

I woke up early this morning and needed to go to the bathroom, so I used my urinal in bed. I thought I was done and removed the urinal and ended up wetting my underwear and the bed. I was frustrated and embarrassed. Later as I thought about it, I realized I have had lack of control of this bladder since about May 26th and this is the first time that I have wet the bed in a while so that's, as my friend Blaine would say, "pretty daggone good." I'll take that. I felt that on Saturday and Sunday I was starting to have increased sensation on the lateral sides of both feet and the fourth and fifth toes of both feet. They have been numb since the first surgery. Well, this morning after I wet the bed, I went in to take a shower and I used the hot water to assess my sensation again. I could feel the hot water on the lateral side of my feet and on my toes which I couldn't feel five days ago. There is another blessing.

The ups and downs just keep coming like waves in the ocean. I need to keep exercising my faith. So simple to teach, so difficult to practice during trials. Luckily, over the years, I have recorded many spiritual blessings and miracles that came after a trial of my faith and learned that sometimes you need to look back to move forward. Look back and read your personal recorded spiritual experiences, blessings, and miracles to help you move forward. The following verses from the Book of Mormon are a great example of the pattern of life. Nephi and his family, his parents, and his brothers and their families as well as the family of Ishmael had a lot of ups and downs as they traveled through the wilderness.

"And it came to pass that we did again take our Journey in the wilderness; and we did travel nearly eastward from that time forth. And we did travel and wade through much affliction in the wilderness; and our women did bear children in the wilderness. And so great were the blessings of the Lord upon us, that while we did live upon raw meat in the wilderness, our women did give plenty of suck for their children, and were strong, yea, even like unto the men; and they began to bear their journeyings without murmurings." (1 Nephi 17: 1-2)

Notes

1 John Lennon, The Beatles

2 Faith is Not Blind by Bruce C. Hafen, Ibid. p. 79-80

5

Be Still My Soul

"I have sometimes thought that we cannot know any man thoroughly well while he is in perfect health. As the ebb-tide discloses the real lines of shore and the bed of the sea, so feebleness, sickness, and pain bring out the real character of a man."[1]

Journal entry June 24, 2021

Accepting the Lord's Will and Panic Attacks

Last night, my son Nick sent a link to a talk Elder Holland gave titled, "Submitting to The Will of the Father," Jan 1989.[2] *That is exactly what the talk was about. The most poignant example was when the Savior asked for the cup to be taken from Him but then said, "Not my will, but Thy will." Then there were Joseph Smith's pleadings to alleviate the sufferings of the Saints and his heartfelt question: "O God, where art Thou? And where is the pavilion that covereth thy hiding place?" (Doctrine and Covenants 121:1)*

I fell asleep listening to it and then early this morning I listened to it again. Then, as I thought about loss of my bowel and bladder functions, I began to feel very anxious. My heart started racing and I started taking rapid breaths. I wanted to sit straight up in bed but could only manage to turn partially on one side and raise up on one elbow. This terrible, out of control feeling continued to intensify, completely taking over. I wanted to run outside before I hyperventilated but I was unable to physically. As my heart continued to race, I realized I was having a panic attack. I had never experienced anything like this. It was terrifying. I was desperate and so I turned to the source I have always turned to in difficult situations. I started pleading for help from Heavenly Father.

As a spelunker I have put myself in positions where I have had to take off my helmet, put one arm forward and one back to my side, turn my head to one side, blow the air out of my chest and then push through a tight squeeze. Over the years I have learned to slow down my breathing to calm down the claustrophobic feeling building in my mind. As I desperately pled for help during this panic attack, I tried to slow my breathing down and gain some control. I started to calm down and as I did, I lay back down and told Heavenly Father I wanted to accept His will, but I would really need His help. Just as I finished praying another panic attack hit me. I felt like I was going to have a heart attack and die.

It was terrible. It was a terrifying feeling. I was out of control and scared. I prayed again and tried slowing my breathing down. I finally calmed down enough to lie back down and decided before my mind took over and I had another panic attack, that I should read from the scriptures. As I read, I was able to keep the extreme anxiety at bay. I could feel that sense of panic just under the surface ready to take over at any moment. Next, I read from the book titled, Led by Divine Design by Elder Rasband. I still felt anxious and on the verge of another panic attack. I had to work at keeping the panic away for the next hour or so. I never wanted to experience a panic attack again.

Breakfast came late. No staff was around to help me get ready to go to my doctor's appointment. I had to get my clothes and towels and put them on my rolling meal cart, then using the walker and while keeping 95% of my weight off my right leg, I used the walker to push the rolling table into the shower area in the bathroom. Before showering, I had to use the bathroom which was no easy task and took several minutes. Because of the delay caused by the panic attacks I didn't get up and started until 9:10 and I was supposed to be picked up at 9:30 to go to the follow up appointment with my surgeon. I felt stressed out between the panic attacks and the rush to get cleaned up and dressed without help. When it rains, it pours. I again felt myself pleading for help. The worst part was that I felt all alone. All I could do was utter a simple prayer from the scriptures, "Lord, I believe; help thou mine unbelief." (Mark 9:24)

They transported me to the hospital in a wheelchair and although I had been concerned about having to sit in the wheelchair and the pain I would suffer, it was not bad at all. My pain was mild. When we arrived, they took me up to the doctor's office on the second floor, checked me in, then rolled me into a room to take x rays. I had to transfer onto the hard table and turn my legs inward, as if pigeon-toed and hold that position during each x ray. It was not easy nor very comfortable. I was so happy to get off that table and back into the wheelchair which is saying a lot considering that I typically dreaded sitting in the wheelchair. After the x-rays they took me into the exam room, and I was able to lie down on the exam table. It was such a great relief to lie down and feel the pain gradually subside. We didn't have to wait very long before the doctor came in. The pain had subsided enough that I was able to sit up on the table and talk to him. We talked very frankly about my bowel and bladder symptoms, and specifically what limitations I was having with numbness and about the numbness in my feet. He showed me the x-rays and said the remaining screw was in a good place and the bone looked good and my fractures on the left side of the pelvis that hadn't been repaired seemed to be healing well. This was all good comforting information, and I was finally able to completely relax after a terribly stressful morning. He stated that in two weeks I could start increasing weight-bearing on the right leg to 25% and over the next month work up to full weight-bearing. He also wrote a recommendation that I be allowed to stay in the care center for two more weeks, due to all the issues I was having.

I am at a much better place right now than I was several hours ago. There was one really good thing that happened this morning and that was meeting Linda at the hospital and seeing her beautiful, happy face. She really helped lift my spirits. She has a gift to lift people that are down and out. I have seen her lift other's spirits so many times and this time it was mine that was lifted.

What a day. This evening, I read two talks by church leaders in the Church of Jesus Christ of Latter-day Saints and wanted to include the excerpts that touched my heart and helped me look at this trial in a better light.

"Frankly, few of us would probably write into our stories the trials that refine us. But don't we love the glorious culmination of a story we read when the protagonist overcomes the struggle? Trials are the elements of the plot that make our favorite stories compelling, timeless, faith promoting, and worthy of telling. The beautiful struggles written into our stories are what draw us closer to the Savior and refine us, making us more like Him." [3]

"Amid the losses we have experienced, there are also some things we have found. Some have found deeper faith in our Heavenly Father and His Son, Jesus Christ. Many have found a fresh perspective on life—even an eternal perspective. You may have found stronger relationships with your loved ones and with the Lord. I hope you have found an increased ability to hear Him and receive personal revelation. Difficult trials often provide opportunities to grow that wouldn't have come in any other way." [4]

The anxiety is now gone. I turned to the source that could help me. I went to sleep with the words of this scripture from the Book of Mormon:

"For behold, I am God; and I am a God of miracles; and I will show unto the world that I am the same yesterday, today, and forever; and I work not among the children of men save it be according to their faith." (2 Nephi 27:23)

Over the years, I had heard many of my patients describe panic attacks, but I really couldn't relate to them until I experienced two, back-to-back. I had no idea how frightening they were. Now I know why they are called panic attacks. What a way to start the day.

Later, as I told Linda about my experience, she said, "You don't panic." Once, after a shoulder surgery in which they had done a nerve block, I went home and, in the evening, my right hand was still numb. I was sitting downstairs watching a movie and out of nowhere a very anxious feeling came over me as I touched my thumb and couldn't feel any sensation. I had to walk outside and take some deep breaths to calm down. That is what I felt this morning but one hundred times more intense and I was a prisoner in my bed. Had I been able to get out of bed and walk outside this morning I think I would have done better.

I now had a new focus with my prayers. My prayer was that a longer stay in the care center would be approved because it would make it so much easier on me while Linda was gone to Oregon to help our son Kyle and his wife Jana take care of our special needs grandson, Mr. Miles, and his little brothers. It would also allow me more time to build up my strength and more time to allow my nerve issues and bowel and bladder functions to start working better. And, if it were the Lord's will, that my bowel and bladder and other issues were not to heal, it would give me more time to come to terms with the idea, accept it and start moving forward.

In the book titled Beyond the Shade of the Mango Tree, I was taught another example on accepting God's will. "For much of the time Mother battled with cancer, she lived with my family and me.

One night I heard her sobbing in her bedroom. Her pain was intense, even after taking her last dose of morphine only two hours earlier.

I entered her room and sobbed with her. I prayed aloud for her to receive instant relief from her pain. And then she did the same thing she had in the field and in the kitchen: she stopped and taught me a lesson. I will never forget her face at that moment: frail, stricken and full of pain, gazing with pity on her sorrowing son. She smiled through her tears, looked directly into my eyes, and said, "It is not up to you or anyone else, but it is up to God whether this pain will go away or not. "

I sat up quietly. She too sat quietly. The scene remains vivid in my mind. That night, through my mother, the Lord taught me a lesson that will stay with me forever. As my mother expressed her acceptance of God's will, I remembered why Jesus Christ suffered in the Garden of Gethsemane and on Golgotha. He said: "Behold I have given unto you my gospel and this is the gospel which I have given unto you—that I came into the world to do the will of my Father, because my Father sent me."

My mother, even in her severe pain, reached out to me, showed me how to accept God's will and helped me to prepare to serve in the Lord's kingdom, under any circumstance. His [Jesus] plaintive plea and His submission to His Father established our way to salvation and set the example for us to follow: "Father, if thou be willing, remove this cup from me: nevertheless, not my will, but thine, be done." [5]

Accepting God's will in extreme trials of faith is a wonderful doctrine but I had never really been in such a desperate situation before. President Russell M. Nelson gave a talk at the October 2020 general conference of the Church of Jesus Christ of Latter-day Saints titled, "Let God Prevail, Embrace the Future, Live a New Normal". It sounded so easy and so right.

"The submission of one's will is really the only uniquely personal thing we have to place on God's altar. The many other things we "give," brothers and sisters, are actually the things He has already given or loaned to us. However, when you and I finally submit ourselves, by letting our individual wills be swallowed up in God's will, then we are really giving something to Him! It is the only possession which is truly ours to give!" [6]

Notes

1 https://www.washingtonpost.com/entertainment/books/candice-millard-on-the-writing-life/2011/09/06/gIQAyPc1UK_story.html , Destiny of the Republic, by Candice Millard

2 Submitting to The Will of the Father, BYU Speeches, Jan 1989 https://speeches.byu.edu/talks/jeffrey-r-holland/will-father

3 Invite Christ to Author Your Story, Camille N. Johnson Primary General President, General Conference October 2021, Church of Jesus Christ of Latter-day Saints

4 What We Are Learning and Will Never Forget, President Russell M. Nelson, President of The Church of Jesus Christ of Latter-day Saints, General conference April 2021, Church of Jesus Christ of Latter-day Saints

5 Beyond the Shade of the Mango Tree, Edward Dube, pg. 88-89

6 Swallowed Up in the Will of the Father, Elder Neal A. Maxwell of the Quorum of the Twelve Apostles, General Conference, October 1995, Church of Jesus Christ of Latter-day Saints

6

"It's Old News"

"Young men, we must give thanks for this day and for every day, no matter how flawed. Bow your heads, give your gratitude to God, and have faith in him, and in a better tomorrow." [1]

I really liked the above quote. It rang true to my ears. I was on the internet one day and saw one of the teaser headlines titled resilience. It also sounded good. These are two excerpts from the article:

"Resilience, defined as the psychological capacity to adapt to stressful circumstances and to bounce back from adverse events, is a highly sought-after personality trait in the modern workplace. As Sheryl Sandberg and Adam Grant argue in their 2017 book, we can think of resilience as a sort of muscle that contracts during good times and expands during bad times."

"In that sense, the best way to develop resilience is through hardship, which various philosophers have pointed out through the years: Seneca noted that "difficulties strengthen the mind, as labor does the body" and Nietzsche famously stated "that which does not kill us, makes us stronger." In a similar vein, the United States Marine Corps uses the "pain is just weakness leaving the body" mantra as part of their hardcore training program." [2]

A neurosurgeon friend, after hearing of the accident, the subsequent surgery, and the severe pain I was experiencing after the surgery, took it upon himself to look at the CT scan taken two weeks after the surgery. We had the following text message exchange:

Neurosurgeon: "Frank, it's Bryson. I pulled up your post op CT scan today. Shep & I looked at it. The long screw was initially placed directly through your sacral spinal canal. Worst possible scenario. Thought you'd want to know."

Frank: "Thank you. Not quite sure what to think getting that news."

Neurosurgeon: "It's old news, and changes nothing about your condition. It is what it is. But it improves your understanding of the events. (Those are the kind of egregious x rays that before digital PACS systems would mysteriously disappear from the radiology dept.) Again, I am sorry you're having to deal with this. Keep your spirit up, work hard at your recovery,"

It is interesting how of all the things he put in the text, that the most important words were, "It's old news." How many times in life do we hang onto the wrongs, the offenses, the mishaps, the tragedies, the mistakes we or others have made and keep our souls anchored down with darkness, despair, and discouragement? We spend so much energy commiserating about the past we can't enjoy the present and look forward to the future.

The following poem by Henry Van Dyke, The Sun-Dial at Wells College, encouraged people to embrace the present moment rather than dwell on the past:

> "The shadow by my finger cast
>
> Divides the future from the past:
>
> Before it, sleeps the unborn hour
>
> In darkness, and beyond thy power:

Behind its unrelenting line,

The vanished hour, no longer thine:

One hour alone is in thy hands, -

The NOW on which the shadow

stands."

For about 2 months after the accident, I spent most of my days and nights lying in bed. It would have been so easy to think about the mistakes that were made and the subsequent consequences which left my life completely upside down. I could have been angry and resentful. Because of a misplaced screw, I had suffered intense bouts of pain for two and a half weeks and once removed left me with nerve damage. I couldn't get up and be active, I slept in 23 hours a day (involuntary clinomania), I missed interactions with family and friends, and I couldn't fulfill my responsibilities as a member of a young single adult ward bishopric. I had no income and didn't know when I would get back to providing an income. The most difficult thing for me was the long separations from my wife Linda and the lonely feeling that came over me as Linda left to drive home from the care center each night. Much as I tried, it was always hard on me. For the most part, I was able to keep a positive attitude but there were still many dark and difficult struggles.

I had plenty of reasons to let myself be filled with darkness, despair, discouragement and even anger but that statement, "It's old news" really helped me look forward rather than dwell in the past. The other part of his statement was also extremely helpful. "Again, I am sorry you're having to deal with this. Keep your spirit up, work hard at your recovery."

These two pieces of advice were key to my recovery. "It's old news" so don't lay around feeling sorry for yourself and make everyone around you miserable and "work hard at your recovery" instead of laying around commiserating the situation. Keeping your sense of humor doesn't hurt either. I laughed as I read this note from a former patient of mine:

P.S. I happen to know there's never been a gray-haired saddle bronc champion, so maybe rethink your second profession!

Early one morning, I read the following verse of scripture: *"Wherefore, be of good cheer, and do not fear, for I the Lord am with you, and will stand by you;"* (Doctrine and Covenants 68:6)

I have read this scripture many times in the past but this time the thought that came to mind after I pondered this verse was that this doesn't mean He (God) changes our circumstances or even rights the wrongs of everyday life. But He brings peace to us in troubled times and in fractured lives to lighten our burden.

"No pain that we suffer, no trial that we experience is wasted. It ministers to our education, to the development of such qualities as patience, faith, fortitude, and humility. All that we suffer and all that we endure, especially when we endure it patiently, builds up our characters, purifies our hearts, expands our souls, and makes us more tender and charitable, more worthy to be called the children of God…and it is through sorrow and suffering, toil and tribulation, that we gain the education that we came here to acquire and which will make us more like our Father and Mother in heaven." [3]

Notes

1 Beneath A Scarlett Sky, by Mark Sullivan, Pg 56, 5th paragraph

2 Resilience, https//hbr.org/ideacast/2017/04/Sheryl-sandberg-and-adam-grant-on-resilience

3 In Kimball, Tragedy or Destiny, 4

7
If Thou Wouldst Have a Blessing of Me....

"The Service you do for others is the rent you pay for your room here on Earth." [1]

Many years ago, I had received a call to visit with President Fred Wasden, my Stake President in the Church of Jesus Christ of Latter-day Saints. I don't remember what was going on in my life on that day, but I had an appointment with him in the evening. That morning, I prayed that I would be up to whatever was coming my way. On my way to the meeting, a thought came to my mind, a thought that was obvious enough, that I wrote it down on a scrap of paper. The thought was, "Serve faithfully if thou wouldst have a blessing of me." I didn't know what the meeting was about or what calling I might be asked to accept but I immediately knew what my answer would be to President Wasden before I ever walked into his office.

> Thought
> Serve faithfully if thou wouldst have a blessing of me.
> November 2013

I found these excerpts about service in a talk titled, The Joy of Service given by Russell C. Taylor

"I can say unashamedly, I rejoice in the service of God. My experience teaches that the highest goodness attainable is a life of unselfish service to mankind. The Master said, "He that is greatest among you shall be your servant." (Matt. 23:11.) It has been wisely said, "Service is the rent we pay for our own room on earth." We should know that the rent is due on a daily basis and know that the receipt is never stamped "paid in full," because the rent, service in God's kingdom, is again due today and due tomorrow.

Some mistakenly think that a commitment to service comes *after* a great spiritual experience. This is like the man who is cold, standing before the stove, and saying, "Give me heat, and *then* I will put in some wood." The joy and blessings of service *follow* the rendering of service." 2

I knew this. My parents had taught me to serve and had been examples of serving others. My wife was always serving people. The following scripture in the Book of Mormon also expressed the importance of service: *"But ye will teach them to walk in the ways of truth and soberness; ye will teach them to love one another, and to serve one another." (Mosiah 4:15)*

Now, fast forward to my stay in the care center or nursing home as I continued recuperating from my pelvic fracture. Overall, physically I was now in a better place. I was still spending the majority of my time in bed, but I could get in and out of bed with minimal pain, I could walk by supporting myself on the walker with both arms and swinging both legs forward at the same time and I was able to go farther and felt like I was getting stronger. I was getting up to go to the bathroom and going to occupational and physical therapy twice a day. I still couldn't tolerate sitting for more than a few minutes at a time. It was too uncomfortable.

Mentally it was a different story. I was worried about how much strain my wife was under, taking care of the house, the yardwork, the garden, finances, being "Gigi" (grandkids name for her) and taking care of the grandkids, and having to find time at the end of very long days to visit me. There were the worries about finances since it would be by my best guess, two months before I could return to work. Two months without a paycheck is not an easy thing to deal with but thanks to a life of faithful paying of tithing and a wise financial advisor, my wife Linda, we were out of debt, which was of some comfort.

Other worries were building. There were mounting medical bills and wondering when I did get back to work if I would be able to perform my regular duties. My job was very physical, and I worried whether I could continue working as a physical therapist without jeopardizing the healing process. Then there were the concerns about not fulfilling my church responsibilities. Bishop Young and Brother Wright were carrying my load.

Up to this point in time I had fallen into what I felt was a good routine. I still woke up early, I would then spend some time pondering, I would often pray vocally, something I had rarely done in the past, and I mean pray from the heart, and then read from the scriptures and books by general authorities. I really couldn't find fault with that routine.

One morning, after pondering, praying, and reading scriptures I changed the routine. I found and listened to a recorded BYU-Idaho devotional by Paul Roberts.

In his talk he discussed four principles, what he called "true principles" of life. I enjoyed his talk. The following are the principles I wrote down:

Principle 1: Remember Hope in Christ

Principle 2: Remember Who You Are

Principle 3: Don't Do It Alone

(I really liked this one and started listening more carefully).

Principle 4: Serve Others[1]

The Holy Ghost touched my heart on this one. Remember the title of this chapter? "If Thou Wouldst Have a Blessing…" But how could I serve lying in bed all day? I pondered this throughout the day but had no answers when I went to bed. In the morning, the answer came sometime during my pondering, praying, and reading the scriptures session. All I had to do was pray. I was certainly in no position to go out and serve others so the opportunities would have to come to me. Then I remembered a talk by Elder Uchtdorf, an apostle in the Church of Jesus Christ of Latter-day Saints. Here was the excerpt that came to mind:

"Some years ago, in our meetinghouse in Darmstadt, Germany, a group of brethren was asked to move a grand piano from the chapel to the adjoining cultural hall, where it was needed for a musical event. None were professional movers, and the task of getting that gravity-friendly instrument through the chapel and into the cultural hall seemed nearly impossible. Everybody knew that this task required not only physical strength but also careful coordination. There were plenty of ideas, but no one could keep the piano balanced correctly. They repositioned the brethren by strength, height, and age over and over again—nothing worked.

As they stood around the piano, uncertain of what to do next, a good friend of mine, Brother Hanno Luschin, spoke up. He said, "Brethren, stand close together and lift where you stand."

It seemed too simple. Nevertheless, each lifted where he stood, and the piano rose from the ground and moved into the cultural hall as if on its own power. That was the answer to the challenge. They merely needed to stand close together and lift where they stood." [4]

For some reason, I accepted this idea with complete confidence. From then on, each morning, I prayed for an opportunity to serve others. I share some of those opportunities that came my way, not to make me look good but to show how Heavenly Father helps us as President Uchtdorf taught to "lift where we stand."

Training for backpacking trip

One of the nurses told me he was preparing to go on a wilderness backpacking trip. He talked about his concerns about how to train to get ready.

Well, backpacking was something I was very experienced at so over the next several weeks I shared some tips for his training, tips that could help him have a successful trip.

Car troubles and money

There was a young lady that came to my room most days to take my meal order. She would often sit down, and we would talk about life. One morning, she came in, took my food order, and then sat down in a chair across from me. She seemed very anxious. I asked her if there was anything I could help her with since during past visits we had talked about what was going on in her life. She told me that she was engaged and that she had recently purchased a car as a surprise for her fiancé. Shortly after purchasing the car, the battery died. She had to buy a new battery which was a big financial strain on her and that is why she was so anxious. She was also angry with the people that sold her the car.

I explained to her that the people at the car dealership didn't want an unsatisfied customer because it would hurt their business. I told her to drive back to the car dealer, explain what had happened and if she did, I told her the dealer would probably reimburse her for the new battery. She took my advice and the next time she came in she was all smiles. I asked why she was so happy. She told me that she had taken my advice and gone back to the dealer and told them about having to purchase a new battery. They reimbursed her for the battery and then they went through and checked some other things on the engine including cleaning a filter. All her anxiety went away, and she was able to enjoy her new car with her fiancé. Other examples were giving physical therapy advice to staff members with aches and pains.

Humor

One of my favorites was to tell "Dad jokes."

"When is a car no longer a car?

When it turns into a driveway."

These are only a few examples of service I was able to provide with little physical effort on my part and yet in serving them I felt better about my situation, and I felt like I was lifted mentally and spiritually.

Gratitude

There was one other form of service that, at the time, I didn't realize was service and that was to be very upbeat and grateful. I made it a point to say "Thank you," every time a staff member helped me with anything. As I did this, I noticed the staff members seemed to be upbeat when they came into my room. Believe me, having worked in hospitals and nursing homes, it is not fun to go into a room with a grumpy, ungrateful patient.

Lesson learned

No matter what belief system you espouse, when you are down and out physically, mentally, or spiritually, and I was experiencing all of these at once, a pity party is of no benefit to you or those around you. I tried to have a few pity parties, but no one wanted to attend let alone be around the guest of honor. I found pity parties wore down my faith and hope and made things worse. Whereas serving others, even a little bit, helped me feel more positive, hopeful, and grateful. And we all know what Heavenly Father thinks about a grateful heart.

Here is a positive outcome from one of my attempts to serve from the confines of my bed. A couple of months after I left the nursing home, my wife and I ran into the nurse that I had given training advice for his back packing trip, while we were shopping in a grocery store. He recognized us and came up to us. I asked him how his backpacking trip turned out. He told us that the first day was a long, difficult hike. They were all exhausted by the time they arrived at their camp that first night. The next morning, everyone was sore and complained of stiff and sore hip muscles. He got up and had no soreness. He had used the walking technique I had told him about that took some of the stress off the hip muscles and made for more efficient hiking. It worked. He was grateful and I felt we had both been blessed. He had served me as a nurse and treated me well. I had given him some hiking advice that was a benefit to him. My service was small, but he was grateful. I learned firsthand that taking Pres Uchtdorf's advice to "lift where you stand," really worked but in my case, I had to modify it to "lift where you lie."

Notes

1 Muhammad Ali,
https://www.brainyquote.com/quotes/muhammad_ali_136676

2 The Joy of Service, By Elder Russell C. Taylor of the First Quorum of the Seventy General Conference October 1984, Church of Jesus Christ of Latter-day Saints

3 Learning the True Principles of Life, Paul Roberts, BYU-Idaho devotional, March 5, 2021

https://www.byui.edu/devotionals/paul-roberts

4 Lift Where You Stand, President Dieter F. Uchtdorf, Second Counselor in the First Presidency of the Church of Jesus Christ of Latter-day Saints, General Conference October 2008

8

Too Many Blessings?

"Pain and suffering are powerful teachers. A wise man once said to me, "I learn the most when I hurt the worst!" [1]

I don't know about you, but I have always thought when injured or after surgery or with a serious illness, that all you needed was one priesthood blessing. [2] I felt that if I had enough faith one blessing should cover everything. When I heard about people with chronic problems that would get multiple priesthood blessings, I wondered if the blessings were helpful. Did the people have enough faith? Were they trying to help themselves or relying completely on the priesthood blessing? Was it okay to ask for multiple blessings?

The day after I fractured my pelvis, my son Nick came to the hospital and gave me a blessing. It was comforting and very specific. While still in the hospital I had a visit from my home ward bishop, Bishop Stucki and for some reason I asked for another priesthood blessing. Two blessings and I was only two weeks into what, unbeknownst to me, was going to be an exceedingly long road to recovery.

After my stay in the hospital, I was discharged to home. Linda and I had been called to serve in a Young Single Adult ward in the Church of Jesus Christ of Latter-day Saints. It was a joint calling. I had been set apart by a member of the stake presidency, but she hadn't. By this time in the healing process, I had had some real setbacks. I seemed to be able to do less and I was experiencing intense bouts of pain more frequently. One morning, I couldn't even raise myself up on my elbows in bed, let alone get up out of bed and was close to calling an ambulance to take me to the hospital. It was becoming unbearable to sit for more than a couple of minutes. I called President Morgan of the Young Single Adult stake presidency and asked him for a priesthood blessing and asked if he could set my wife apart. They came and President Peterson gave Linda a wonderful blessing and set her apart in her church calling and then President Morgan gave me a blessing. Wow, I was now up to three priesthood blessings. What was wrong with me? Was my faith so weak that one blessing wasn't enough? Were my desires selfish? Were my desires and will clashing with Heavenly Father's will?

In mid-July, I returned to church for the first time and on August 2nd, I returned to work. It was difficult. I had been basically bedbound for two months, sitting for any amount of time was painful and trying to stay up all day either sitting or standing at work was a real challenge mentally and physically. Well, you guessed it. I asked Bishop Young, who I was serving with in a young single adult ward bishopric, for a priesthood blessing. What was wrong with me, four priesthood blessings. I was now one of those people who had multiple blessings for the same thing. Was I faithless or faithful? Was I over doing it with the priesthood blessings? Was my faith so feeble that one priesthood blessing wouldn't take care of everything?

Fast forward to December 13, 2021. I had been working since the beginning of August, I was alternating between swimming, exercising every other day, and I was fulfilling my church and home responsibilities. I was, however, still having pain in my right sacroiliac joint. The joint that connects the pelvis to the spine. I was swimming as much as one mile, but I could only use my legs to kick for about twelve to fourteen of the thirty-six laps. If I kicked for more laps, I would have more pain in the sacroiliac joint and groin muscles. Three months before, Linda and I had hiked the Kathryn Lake trail at Brighton ski resort. It was about a 4-mile hike and Linda kept us going at a good pace. I was scared I would pay a price for that first hike, but I was fine. A month and a half later, I went for a short hike in the foothills east of Layton and twenty minutes into the hike the sacroiliac joint pain came on and a few minutes later the groin pain started. I was going backwards with the healing process.

After that hike I started to cut back on my exercise routine. The more I thought about it, the more I came to believe that because there was a screw though the middle of a joint that has some movement, it was limiting the movement and putting more strain on the muscles in the groin. My hip flexors were being overstrained. On October 26, 2021, I had an appointment with the doctor. He took new x rays, which showed that the screw was intact and hadn't backed out. He agreed that the screw was probably causing hypomobility of the joint and putting an excess stress on the muscles.

He suggested we wait 6 months and then, if it was still a problem, remove it. It had been 5 months since the surgery. I told him if I waited until the next year, it would cost me our large insurance deductible and we had met the deductible for the year 2021 and I wanted to have it taken out before the end of the year. My other thought was that the longer the joint was immobile the more likely it would create other problems in the future. He agreed and we set the surgery date for December 14, 2021. I had the pre-op visit on Monday, December 6th. I had a Covid test on December 11th and then on December 12th, we had our sons Nick and Eric and their families over for dinner. That evening, before they left, Linda asked them to give me a blessing. I hadn't thought of asking for a blessing. Yep, one more priesthood blessing, number five to be exact.

As I have pondered all these blessings, my perspective has changed. I have concluded that having multiple priesthood blessings was not only appropriate but very much needed. I went back and reviewed my journal entries. I had recorded each priesthood blessing, the important things contained in each one and what the circumstances were each time I had another blessing. Each blessing was very distinct, very different, and very specific to my needs at each of the times I asked for them.

Blessing Number One

My son Nick gave me this blessing on May 23rd, before I had the surgery to stabilize the pelvic fractures. There were three very specific things he blessed me with. He blessed me that I would have increased faith in Christ, that I was being further refined by this trial and would grow from it and my work would be okay.

(I was very concerned about not working and finances).

Blessing Number Two

On May 28th, I asked Bishop Stucki for a blessing when he visited me in the hospital. There were some wonderful words in this blessing. In his blessing he stated that "as you recognize miracles, miracles will become more prevalent in your mind, your faith will be strengthened, the Lord is aware of you." He closed the blessing stating that "he was sealing this priesthood blessing and it was as if the Lord was doing it personally" and then he closed in the name of Jesus Christ. This last statement went right to my heart.

(This day was possibly my worst day in the hospital. I woke up in the morning with intense burning pain down the back of my left thigh and into my groin. I became "shocky" walking to the therapy gym, did some therapy and felt "shocky" again. They had me lie down on a harder low table to recover and then I had to roll on my left side with the unhealed fractures to get up which was terribly painful. Walking back to my room I was chastised by the doctor, which in turn upset Linda and she walked away leaving me standing with the doctor

and feeling alone. I didn't blame her. She was just going by what the doctor was telling us. As a self-employed physical therapist, when injured in the past I had to push myself harder because I had to get back to work as soon as I could. As I watched Linda walk away, I felt all alone. I felt terrible. This time, I was only doing what the therapists had asked me to do. I was also still confused by the fact that even when the terrible nerve pain was present while sitting, walking didn't usually bother me. After a short rest from physical therapy, I had occupational therapy, but while waiting for them I was in intense pain sitting in the wheelchair. They then took me down for x-rays.

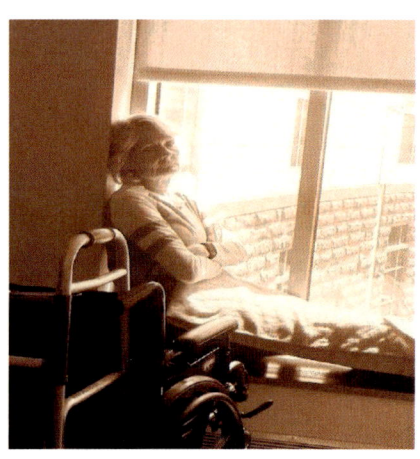

Linda taking a mental break after hearing the doctor tell me I was pushing too hard.

It was about this point in time that a thought entered my mind. I wondered if one of the screws might be hitting a nerve. I pushed it aside because I couldn't understand why if a screw were pressing on a nerve the pain was not constant. After being chastised by the doctor and seeing how it had upset Linda, I decided to self-limit my activity no matter what the therapists wanted me to do.

There were a few other things that happened that day. Twice, after raising the head of the bed, I lost control of my bladder and wet the bed. Later in the afternoon, after sitting on the toilet, I got up thinking I was done and had an accident on the floor. The doctor was told about this loss of bladder control and came in and did some sensation testing on my lower legs, some strength testing on my feet and toes and then he did a straight leg raising test with my left leg and lowered it quickly, causing me to cry out as a pain shot from my left upper thigh and buttocks into my groin. It was a terribly difficult day physically, emotionally, mentally, and spiritually).

Blessing Number Three

On June 2nd, this blessing was given to me by President Morgan of the young single adult stake presidency. It came at my request because after I was discharged from the hospital the struggle with pain was becoming more intense each day. In the blessing, these were the words that touched my spirit: "I needed or would be able to recognize and follow the promptings of the Holy Ghost and I would heal and on the other side of this trial I would learn lessons." *(I didn't realize until after I pondered the words of his blessing that I had been praying for a miracle on my timeline not Heavenly Father's timeline. I spent a couple of hours late that night repenting of trying to force my will on Heavenly Father rather than accept His will.)*

Blessing Number Four

August 1st was Fast Sunday and my second Sunday back in the young single adult ward. On this day, I was given the fourth priesthood blessing by Bishop Young and his First counselor, Ron Wright. I was struggling to return to church activity and return to work. The following were the words that stood out in my mind: I was blessed to continue healing, and not to be angry.*(This was important because as I returned to work and church activities it was physically difficult. My job was breaking down my body and was going to slow down my healing process or worse, set me backwards and make it so I couldn't work or be active in life. The other part that was even more important was not to be angry.*

I was told by so many people, including anesthesiologists and neurosurgeons that knew me, that they were angry at the surgeon that had made the mistake of placing the long screw through the sacral spinal canal damaging the lower spinal nerves and never following up with me once I started complaining of loss of bladder control. I can honestly say, I never once felt anger and didn't want to waste any mental or spiritual energy on being angry. As my neurosurgeon told me, "It's old news." I was so thankful for that reinforcing statement.)

Blessing Number Five

It was given on December 12th. Here is the background for this blessing. The two weeks before my third surgery was very stressful. We had been around our grandkids who were really sick with bad coughs, ear infections and runny noses. I was concerned about getting the Covid virus. The husband of one of my co-workers had tested positive for Covid. If I got sick, my chance to have the screw removed would be lost. I would have to wait until the next year and would have to pay the high deductible following the surgery. New stresses, another priesthood blessing.

(This time, my sons Eric and Nick gave me the blessing. The statement that stood out in my mind was one in which Eric blessed me with assurance. Assurance that the surgeon would be guided and blessed to perform the surgery correctly. I didn't realize how important this was until they were walking me back to the pre-op room to have me change into a hospital gown and hook me up to an IV line. I couldn't believe how calm I was. I felt relaxed and wasn't worried. As we walked past the first pre-op room, I turned my head and glanced into the room and suddenly had a flashback memory.

It was the room where I had my first pre-op preparation prior to the surgery that placed a screw through my sacral spinal canal leaving me with tremendous pain for two weeks and continued nerve damage. As I lay in the pre-op room that thought came to mind, and I was suddenly very emotional and upset. I talked to Linda for a few minutes and was able to calm down. The words of the priesthood blessing, "assurance that the surgeon would be blessed and guided" came to mind and helped comfort me and calm my emotions. After the surgeon came in and talked to us, I was so calm I almost fell asleep waiting to be taken to the operating room.)

As I look back, I have a new perspective on priesthood blessings. I still feel that in most cases, one priesthood blessing is enough. In the past, I have had priesthood blessings for assorted reasons, and one was always sufficient. Excruciating pain, concerns of healing, concerns about the load Linda was carrying, loss of income and health insurance, and multiple surgeries were all struggles I had faced, and the multiple blessings seemed appropriate to me. I still don't have an answer as to whether one can have too many priesthood blessings. Each one came at a time when I was struggling with new and different challenges. Each came when I was doing everything I could do but it wasn't enough. The statements in each were quite different, and specific to what was going on at the time. Most importantly, each was answered, and specific blessings were received that gave me hope and the strength needed to keep going and not give up. I am so glad I recorded each blessing. I can honestly testify that Heavenly Father was involved in the details of my life.

Notes

1 The Savior's Final Week, Andrew C. Skinner Pg 99

2 Priesthood blessing: Priesthood blessings are given by the authority of the priesthood for healing, comfort, and encouragement. Priesthood Ordinances and Blessings, https://www.churchofjesuschrist.org/study/manual/family-guidebook/priesthood-ordinances...

9

Ministering Angels

"From the beginning down through the dispensations God has used ministering angels as His emissaries in conveying love and concern for His children…When we speak of those that are instruments in the hand of God, we are reminded that not all angels are from the other side of the veil. Some of them we walk with and talk with--- here, every day." [1]

Because of this injury, I have been given a new insight into the Savior's words as recorded in the following scripture verse:

"Then shall the righteous answer him, saying, Lord, when saw we thee an hungered, and fed thee? or thirsty, and gave thee drink?

"When saw we thee a stranger, and took thee in? or naked, and clothed thee?

"Or when saw we thee sick, or in prison, and came unto thee?

"And the King shall answer and say unto them, Verily I say unto you, inasmuch as ye have done it unto one of the least of these my brethren, ye have done it unto me." (Matthew 25: 37-40)

This book wouldn't be complete without recounting the ministering that was done on my behalf. The ministering angels blessed my wife Linda's and my life. This was where the ministering angels hit the ground running and didn't stop until they knew we were back on our feet again. I wish I could share the name of every person and the service they provided but that would fill up another book. Having said that, I have recorded all their names and deeds in my "Grateful Journal."

Mental Ministering

People that know me well have heard me describe the five squirrels that are running around inside my head. The words "ponder" and "meditate" strike fear in my heart. My thoughts change as quickly as five squirrels jumping from branch to branch in a tree. Wondering how I was going to survive mentally as I thought about being stuck in my bed all day and all night for a prolonged period was a huge concern. Sleeping in, to me, is staying in bed until 6:00 a.m. with my eyes open wondering why I am still in bed. How would I keep my sanity? It was like my version of the Movie, "Ground Hog Day" where Bill Murray would go to sleep each night and, in the morning, wake up to the same exact day and conditions as the day before. Each morning, I woke up to the same scenario. If I am doing something very mentally or physically challenging the squirrels are quiet and I can concentrate, which is one reason I like hard, challenging physical hobbies. I can relate to the late Alpinist, Marc-Andre Leclerc who said, "I never felt that Squirrel brained twitchy stuff when I was climbing." [2, 2a, 2b]

Books and more books

I am an avid reader, and television had no interest for me. Without being asked, and without knowing my passion for reading books, real books, books that you can hold and turn pages, people brought me books that were their favorite or books they thought I would like. At the height of my book reading, I was reading five different books each day. For example, there were the scriptures, then "Led by Devine Design" by Elder Rasband, "Faith is Not Blind" by

Bruce C. and Marie K. Hafen, Destiny of The Republic, a book about President Garfield's assassination, "Buried In The Sky" a book about Sherpa climbers on K2, etc. As I finished one book other books would be provided. I remember one Friday morning, after having finished several books, I was concerned about running out of books to read. I thought that I would go crazy staring at the ceiling or out the window all day without a book to read. Linda was in Oregon for ten days and I was stuck in the care center. I prayed someone would bring me more books and the next day, two good friends, Blaine Austin and my bishop, Darcel Stucki, brought me more books.

Word Search and Crossword Puzzles

There was a young lady that was an employee of the care center. She was the activity director. One day she brought me in some pages with Crossword puzzles and Word Search puzzles. I thanked her for them and immediately set about solving them. The next morning, she came in and was surprised that I had completed all the puzzles. I thanked her for bringing them to me and let her know how much they helped pass the time. From that day forward, she made it a point to bring me puzzles every day and if she was off for a day, she had others bring me puzzles. Towards the end of my stay, she dropped off a 175-page book of puzzles. What a blessing she was in my life. These were just a few examples of ministering angels that helped take my mind off my struggles.

Puzzles and Racko

My sister Diana came and worked on a puzzle I had set up and had little patience for and then she also brought the game Racko and played it with Linda and me. My friend, Doug Shepherd, dropped off a really challenging puzzle. I couldn't sit very long and when staff members or visitors came by I had them work on the puzzle. It took a long time to finish this puzzle, in fact, I finished it the night before I was discharged to home. The frustrating thing was that the very center piece was missing. It was not on the floor, under the furniture, it was missing. Linda, being a creative soul, cut out a piece of paper the shape of the missing piece and then colored it black and fit it into the puzzle. The challenge took my mind off my problems.

Physical Ministering

I was often genuinely concerned about the load my wife now carried. I felt stressed about the need for the lawn to be mowed and edged, the garden needing to be watered and the fruit trees needing to be sprayed, typically my spring and summer tasks. Now the burden was on her shoulders.

My elder's quorum president, who is also my primary care doctor, Richard Hall, stopped by the house one evening. At this time, I still had the misplaced screw in the sacral spinal canal causing me tremendous pain when I tried to sit for more than a couple of minutes. He spent an hour discussing my medical issues. He then went home, picked up his daughter Heather, and they came back and edged and mowed our lawn even though he was scheduled to leave on a vacation for Texas the next day. While on vacation he checked up on me and was even instrumental in getting approval for me to be admitted to a care center, again doing it while on vacation. Our ministering brothers Bob and Jack Lowe then stepped in and took over edging and mowing the lawn and when they couldn't do it, they had others step in. Some brothers sprayed my fruit trees. Our friend, Diane Austin, brought a wheelchair to the house. My friend, Bruce Abbott, removed the toilet seat so that the special toilet chair could be put in place, and he also took the doors off the bathroom and bedroom so the wheelchair would fit through the doors. Members of our young single adult ward planned a Family Home Evening activity at our home. They weeded our garden, washed, and detailed our vehicles and when I called my wife at 10:15 p.m. from the care center, they were still there having fun and surrounding her in love. Another experience with the young single adults occurred the first Sunday when I returned to church with our young single adults. I recorded it in my journal.

Journal Entry 7/18/2021

I decided I would go to bishopric meeting this morning and then sacrament meeting. I was scheduled to give the thought for bishopric meeting. I usually try to get it out of the church handbook, but as I was praying and thinking about what section to read from a scripture came to mind. It's found in the book of John in the New Testament.

"Peace I leave with you, my peace I give unto you: not as the world giveth, give I unto you. Let not your heart be troubled, neither let it be afraid." (John 14:27)

I realized that although this was not the church handbook, this is one of our main handbooks in the church, the scriptures. It was nice being back in a bishopric meeting. Afterwards, I decided to stay for Ward Council. I surprised the members of the council when I walked into the meeting and sat down. It was nice to be back. By the end of that meeting, my bottom was achy. I went home with the intention of lying down until sacrament meeting, but after eating breakfast with Linda I went back to the church to help prepare for the meeting. Several of the young single adults were there when I walked in, and they seemed happy and excited to see me, which made me feel good to be back.

The bishop conducted the meeting. He stood up to announce the speakers and then without any warning asked me to spend a couple of minutes and share a few thoughts with the ward. I got up and shared the scripture John 14:27, bore my testimony and sat down. After sacrament meeting, I was going to go home but I decided to stay for Sunday School. I walked to the Sunday School room and saw the hard, metal chairs and muttered that there was no way I was going to sit on those chairs. Two of the young single adult sisters heard my comment, immediately got up, walked down to the foyer, picked up a heavy chair that was padded and brought it into the Sunday School room for me to sit on. I felt grateful to them and was able to enjoy the class as the chair was amazingly comfortable.

Prayer

Prayers were another form of ministering. How many times when an accident, illness, tragedy or death happen in someone's life do we say "I wish I knew what I could do to help you" or "I wish I could do more for you. I guess I can pray". I've said this many times over the years, as if prayer was a consolation prize and not that important. We were grateful for the many prayers that were offered on our behalf were. There were many members of the Church of Jesus Christ of Latter-day Saints that put our names on the temple prayer rolls. There were prayers in church and personal prayers said on our behalf. A friend of mine, Charlie Parker, told his wife, Sandie, about my injury and the difficult recovery I was experiencing and she stopped by and asked if she could put my name on the Prayer Warrior list. The thought that crossed my mind when she asked was, "Yes! I need all the prayers I can get." I was surprised how her offer to add me to a prayer list of people I had never met, and would probably never meet, lifted my spirits. Never discount the power of prayer and how it can lift and comfort people during hard trials.

Spiritual Ministering

There were so many examples of spiritual ministering, besides the multiple priesthood blessings, that I could fill up a book with them. Rather than do so, I want to share one specific experience because of how it blessed me but also the spiritual insight it taught me.

It was a Saturday evening. My friend, Blaine Austin, stopped by to visit. I was lying on the bed in our guest bedroom. It is a smaller room and there is not a chair in the room, just the bed and a window seat. Blaine sat down in the window seat, and we talked for a half hour or so. It wasn't comfortable on his back, so he laid down on the bed next to me. We continued to talk about family, politics, religion, books, etc. It was so nice to have company. Towards the end of the visit, he admitted that it was the Saturday evening session of stake conference, but he had chosen to visit me rather than attend the meeting. Now some might criticize his choice. But it reminded me of a story about Abraham Lincoln.

In 1865, President Lincoln, arrived back in the capitol after having been in Richmond. When he arrived, he didn't go home, didn't go report his good news that the war was over to the War Department but rather went straight to the home of his good and loyal friend, William Seward. Seward was bed bound and recovering from a carriage accident that had nearly cost his life. "He couldn't wait to visit his convalescing friend to tell him firsthand of the events at Richmond and to celebrate the end of the war. According to Seward's son, Lincoln spoke gently to his still critical and suffering father, casually stretching his elongated body out on Seward's bed with his hand supporting his tilted head. Lincoln stayed, conversing, and encouraging, until his loyal friend and secretary of State had drifted off to sleep." [3]

Blaine had an important meeting to attend, one that could have blessed him spiritually. Lincoln had especially important news for the War Department and had been away from his family. Both men, chose to serve their friends over their needs. Now for the spiritual insight. In the King James bible, in the book of Luke, Jesus teaches this important lesson:

38 Now it came to pass, as they went, that he entered into a certain village: and a certain woman named Martha received him into her house.

39 And she had a sister called Mary, which also sat at Jesus' feet, and heard his word.

40 But Martha was cumbered about much serving, and came to him, and said, Lord, dost thou not care that my sister hath left me to serve alone? Bid her therefore that she help me.

41 And Jesus answered and said unto her, Martha, Martha, thou art careful and troubled about many things:

42 But one thing is needful: and Mary hath chosen that good part, which shall not be taken away from her. (Luke 10: 38-42)

Martha was doing good things. She was preparing a meal and trying to make the Savior comfortable. The problem was that she was judging Mary who was providing a different service. Mary was listening to the Savior. Both were valid services. The thought that came to my mind was that we all have different talents and gifts and so we serve differently but just because one person bakes cookies or cleans the house or does yard work doesn't mean their service is better than someone lending a listening ear. They are all good services. Blaine could have gone to the Saturday evening church session, but he chose to visit his friend. Was it a valid service? Yes. Spending those two hours with me lifted my spirits. It took my mind off my pain and troubles and worries.

Ministering angels saved me mentally, lifted me spiritually and allowed me to heal physically. They took care of obvious and not so obvious needs, taking some of the load off Linda's shoulders and allowing me to rest, knowing they were taking care of us as Heavenly Father's ministering angels.

Notes

1 Jeffrey R. Holland, "The Ministry of Angels," Elder Jeffrey R. Holland of the Quorum of the Twelve Apostles, General Conference October 2008, Church of Jesus Christ of Latter-day Saints

2 Live Fast, Die Young: The Story of Marc-Andre Leclerc

2a The Alpinist, 2021 Documentary

2b The Psychology of a Free Solo Climber

3 The Covenant, Lincoln and the War, Timothy Ballard, pg. 316

10

Don't Look Down

" Give ear to my words, O Lord, consider my meditation. Hearken unto the voice of my cry, my King, and my God: for unto thee will I pray. My voice shalt thou hear in the morning, O Lord; in the morning will I direct my prayer unto thee, and will look up."
(Psalms 5: 1-3)

    As a physical therapist, one area I specialized in was balance and vestibular dysfunction. This area of treatment encompasses a wide variety of diagnoses, symptoms and affects young and old. It involves treatment of balance issues due to concussions, disease, and age-related problems. A common habit of people with balance problems is, while walking, they look down at their feet. They are afraid of tripping and falling down. They don't trust their balance and feel safer looking down as they take each hesitant step. If they watch the ground and where they are placing their feet, they assume they will be safer.

    In the clinic, after performing a thorough evaluation to determine the specific cause of their balance issues, whether it be inner ears, eyes or somatosensory (feet on the ground) issues or some combination of the three, a program specific to their needs is created, and therapy begins.

One frequent problem I have had to correct with many people over the years is the problem of looking down at their feet. In my clinic I have an overhead rail system and inside the rail is a small four wheeled dolly that rolls along the track. I attach a short length of 9mm static climbing rope with a carabiner attached to the dolly. The patient is fitted with a harness and then the carabiner is attached to the back of the harness. This provides patients with a safety mechanism which allows them to work on walking, without the fear of falling. They can stumble a little but cannot fall.

As we begin working on walking balance, one of the first things we have them do is to take more determined steps rather than hesitant steps. Sometimes this may entail taking a longer stride or it may be as simple as increasing their walking speed. Often, they are pleased to be walking with more confidence, but they are still looking down as they walk and have difficulty maintaining their balance. The problem with looking down at your feet is that you do not really see where you are going, or what obstacles are ahead of you until it is too late. You tend to deviate from walking a straight line and it makes you more unsteady, and more likely to trip, lose your balance and fall.

I remember as a teenager trying to ride my bike along a painted line on the side of the road. I would start pedaling and then look down at the line directly in front of the front tire. It was nearly impossible to keep my tire rolling down the painted line. I soon discovered that if I looked up a little and focused my eyes about 20-30 feet out in front of the tire, I was able to stay on the line 90% of the time. Can you imagine a tight rope walker looking straight down at his feet? The key to balancing is keeping their eyes up. They would have great difficulty maintaining their balance if they looked down at their feet all the time.

In the October 2011 general conference of The Church of Jesus Christ of Latter-day Saints, Elder Clark B. Cook, of the Seventy, told of an experience he had during his first week as a General Authority. It had been a particularly tiring week, his briefcase was overloaded, and his mind preoccupied with this question: "How can I possibly do this? "As he stepped onto the elevator, his head was down, and he stared at the floor.

The elevator stopped on another floor and someone else got on. Elder Cook didn't look up to see who it was. As the door closed, the person asked, "What are you looking at down there?"

Elder Cook instantly recognized President Thomas S. Monson's voice. He looked up and responded, "Oh, nothing."

President Monson smiled, pointed heavenward and lovingly suggested, "It is better to look up!" As the elevator continued downward, President Monson explained that he was on his way to the temple.

They both got off the elevator and parted ways. Elder Cook said this, "When he bid me farewell, his parting glance spoke again to my heart, "Now, remember, it is better to look up.'"[1]

Here is an example of needing to look up when I felt like I had no more in me to give. It really shows the ups and downs of healing we sometimes must go through.

The Roller Coaster of Healing

It was a Friday evening in August, and I had mowed our front lawn for the first time since mid-May. I felt surprisingly good. Saturday morning, when I woke up, I felt like I had been run over by a truck. I sent a phone text to our ministering brothers (men assigned to help families in the church with their needs) to see if they could help with the back lawn because I was in rough shape. They were at the lake boating and said they would come in the afternoon.

Linda was out of town, I was tired and sore, it had been a stressful week at work as I had been informed that the other physical therapist that I worked with was quitting five weeks earlier than we had agreed upon and his last day was the end of the upcoming work week. I was already struggling with treating only 30% of the patients and didn't know how I would take over all the patients.

I decided to just keep mowing. While mowing the lawn, underneath one of our fruit trees, I ran into a branch, hitting my head hard enough that it broke the skin. I reached up to rub the painful spot and when I looked at my fingers there was a good amount of blood on them. It was the last straw. I dropped to my knees, alone in the back yard and started praying and pleading for help. I needed something to go right. I didn't need more pain. My body hurt, my head hurt, I was tired and sore, I was feeling the stress of work and losing my help, and I was in desperate need of comfort. After my prayer, I felt better, and I stood up and finished mowing the lawn and then completed several other yard and house chores I had hoped to complete before Linda came home from Oregon.

Late in the afternoon, I decided I wanted to hike the dirt trail along the side of Hobbs Pond. I started on the south side, where there is a small boat ramp. It felt good to be hiking again. I walked at a casual pace. As I got to the east side of the pond, it was very green, there were a lot of ferns along the side of the trail, the air was filled with the sound of crickets and birds, and I was all alone, and it was wonderful to be out in nature again.

At one point on the trail, I hiked down a small hill, crossed a stream and stopped by a large tree that had been cut or had fallen down. As I stood there, it was very peaceful and I suddenly realized how much physical labor I had done throughout the day, that I was hiking for the first time in months, and I was in the beautiful outdoors. Two weeks prior to this, I couldn't have even done 25% of what I had done that day let alone go for a hike afterwards.

I stopped and sat down on the dead log. I was overwhelmed with gratitude and guilt. I started praying, and not just the habitual prayer you offer before you climb in bed, but a very earnest and heartfelt prayer. I prayed for forgiveness for giving into feelings of hopelessness, for being impatient, for wanting to give up and quit, for forgetting all the miracles and blessings I had written down every day since being injured. I was reminded of all the blessings and little miracles I had received as they came flooding back into my mind and heart. It was spiritually healing, and I knew I could keep going.

I got home and while talking to our neighbors, the Bouwhuises, it started raining. We were in a drought. I looked up, grinned, raised my hands overhead and told them it was a blessed day. After talking with them I walked across the street to my home, and as I walked up the wet driveway, there was a little snake trying to wiggle its way to the lawn. I picked it up thinking it was a Garter snake. Suddenly it flipped its head around and latched onto my knuckle with its teeth, and I realized it was probably not a Garter snake. For some reason I started smiling even more. The wind was picking up, so I went into the backyard and picked the beautiful, palm-sized peaches we had been blessed with, before they were blown off the tree. I was looking up again.

"Trust in the Lord with all thine heart; and lean not unto thine own understanding. In all thy ways acknowledge him, and he shall direct thy paths." (Proverbs 3: 5-6)

Don't look down:

Tightrope walker completes 2,198-foot walk from Eiffel Tower Nathan Paulin walked about two hundred feet off the ground, crossing the Seine River between the Eiffel Tower and the Chaillot theatre in Paris.

Looking Up

Mary was sad until she looked up and saw the Savior at the Garden tomb. The children of Israel were saved from the poison of the serpents by simply looking up at the Brass Serpent. Those that wouldn't look up suffered needlessly.

"God made suffering a required course in life, but growth had to be an elective. Christ didn't perform the Atonement to free us from suffering but to be able to be with us in our suffering. The goal was that we would be comforted not comfortable. Progress and growth are seldom comfortable, but they are always worth it. The Atonement of Christ is not only about overcoming death and sin. The Lord also carried our pains, sicknesses, mistakes, and heartaches. Because he descended below them all, He can offer consolation and comfort during challenges, perspective and peace during trials, and divine assistance through it all." [2]

Sometimes we wonder why Heavenly Father allows things to happen to people. Personally, I have come to believe it is to get our attention and to give us the opportunity to improve. I believe Heavenly Father knows each one of us intimately and knows what each of us needs to help us make changes that will make us better people. For some people, a thought that they need to change something in their life is enough, for some it might be losing a job, for others it might be the death of a loved one. I believe, for me, it was an injury significant enough to turn my entire life upside down. Something that affected me mentally, emotionally, physically, and spiritually.

The third priesthood blessing given to me by President Morgan included the statement, "I would heal and on the other side of this trial I would learn lessons." I am now far enough along in this trial that I am learning lessons. It is important to ponder, pray and read from the scriptures and other good books. It is important to take time to stop and look up. I needed to look up to see all the ministering angels in my life. Look up to see who needed my help and ministering efforts. In my case, it was especially important to look up to my Heavenly Father with gratitude. Gratitude that He knows me and knows what I need to start transforming me into something better. Look up to the source of all blessings.

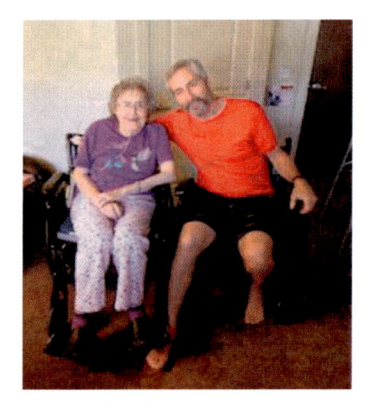

Mom and I share a warm reunion in our wheelchairs at the care center

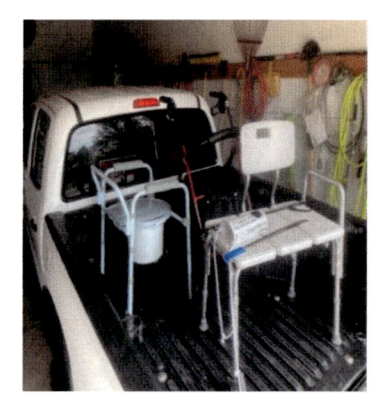

Time to return all the adaptive equipment

I have done a lot of physically challenging adventures that taught me I could do hard things and not give up, but this challenge pushed me to the limit. Will I make it through this trial? Yes. Do I still have some challenges as far as healing? Yes. Will I be completely healed from the injury? I really don't know. Is Heavenly Father aware of me and my needs? Yes. How do I know that everything will work out according to my Heavenly Father's will? Because, through this trial I have learned to look up.

His Eye Is on the Sparrow

Whenever I am tempted,
Whenever clouds arise,
When songs give place to sighing,
When hope within me dies,
I draw the closer to Him,
From care He sets me free;
His eye is on the sparrow,
And I know He cares for me;
His eye is on the sparrow,
And I know He cares for me.
by C. D. Martin

Pushing my limits climbing Denali 2014

Joy of not quitting and summiting Ben Lomond Peak at Sunrise 2020

Notes

1 Look Up My Soul the Divine Promise of Hope, Gerald N. Lund, pg. xi
2 Brad Wilcox, "Because of the Messiah in a Manger", pages xii-xiii.

Epilogue

"Faith is not an inheritance; it is a choice." [1]

It has been eight months and two days since the accident. Last night, I decided it was time to take on the challenge of skinning to the top of Snow Basin Ski resort. It requires a lot of endurance and determination. Two miles of hiking up the hills of a ski resort. There is a reason most people ride the ski lifts to the top of the mountain. I got my gear together and loaded it into the car. I then proceeded to have a long night with very little sleep. Thoughts like "I am too tired, I am not strong enough, what if I fall skiing down the mountain in the dark and hurt myself, kept cycling through my mind and then… it was time. My alarm went off. I was so tired I thought about putting it off for another day. It was 3:50 a.m. in the morning and I guess my habit over many years of early morning adventures took over and I found myself, with all my doubts and worries, getting up, putting on my winter clothes and heading out to the car. Just like I had so many times over the years. Only this time I had more to prove to myself. People that know me know a phrase I coined many years ago. It is "sissybedwetter." The last thing I wanted to do was quit part way up the mountain and then have to label myself a "sissybedwetter."

I got in the car, started the engine and I was off for one of my biggest mental and physical challenges in a long time. Once I started driving, I felt more determined. I played songs from The Piano Guys as I drove through the early morning darkness. It helped push aside the worries and doubts. As I entered the mouth of Weber Canyon, the strong wind pouring down from the top of the mountain shook my car and I wondered if I would have to battle strong, cold winds as I skinned up the mountain. I kept driving. I arrived at the parking lot of Snow Basin ski resort and there was only one other car other than employee cars. I parked the car, got out and changed into my skinning ski boots. It was cold so I zipped up my windbreaker and pulled the hood over my head. I grabbed my pack and skis, checked my headlamp, made sure I had the required blue band and that the flashing red light on the back of my pack was working. I walked between the buildings of the main lodge and stepped onto the snow next to the Needles Tram. Once my skis were on there was no more hesitation. I was going for the top. I was the second person to start the journey this morning. It was 4:45 a.m. I couldn't see the lights on the first skinner ahead of me, but I could see a single set of ski tracks heading off into the dark. At that moment, it didn't cross my mind that I might catch the first skinner. It wasn't my goal for the morning climb. I put my head down and started to follow his tracks up the mountain while trying to find my own rhythm.

Once I started, it didn't take long to find a comfortable pace. Soon, I found myself at the base of School Hill looking up at a long, steep climb. The first skier had bypassed School Hill and took the cat track off to the left which is an easier climb, an easier grade, and a longer traverse but one many less experienced people choose instead of taking on the daunting School Hill. I stopped, bent over, and rotated the back of the bindings so that they lifted the heels of my boots to give my boot heels more height and to save energy as I skinned up the hill. It really felt steep, and I was tired but as I reached the top of School Hill, I felt more hope that I could do this. I could see the lights of the first skinner. He was just starting up Bear Hollow. I was content to keep skinning at my pace, keep climbing and not worry about catching up to him.

It was a beautiful morning. Although the moon was just a half-moon, it was bright enough to cast very detailed shadows of the tall pine trees on the snow in front of me. I couldn't help but smile and be grateful for such a beautiful morning. Every few minutes I looked up and realized that although he had had at least a quarter mile lead on me when I started, I was steadily catching up. A few hundred feet below Middle Bowl, I caught up to him as he was resting, said hello, and left him standing there apparently catching his breath.

I had skinned up to Middle Bowl two weeks before. I had turned around not wanting to overdo it and not wanting to set myself backwards and knowing full well that the rest of the climb from there to the top was the more challenging part of the route. With my weak right leg, I didn't feel comfortable tackling the hills above at that time.

Today, I was determined to climb to the top. The next two hills and gradual slopes challenged me, but I felt I could keep going. The second to the last hill is the steepest hill in the climb, with the face getting steeper at the top. When the snow is icy or when drifting snow has been blown across the groomed face it can be difficult to prevent the skis from losing traction and sliding backwards but I have found that putting more pressure on the heels of the ski boots to keep more pressure on more of the surface area of the skins attached to the skis helps. It takes good arm strength as well using the poles to prevent the skis from sliding backwards on the steep slope. As I started up the hill, a very strong headwind blew right in my face. I had to zip my jacket all the way up to keep the hood from blowing off. The wind was strong enough that it shook my body. Towards the top third of the hill the wind had blown drifting snow across the groomed snow and my skis started to slide backwards. Between the skis sliding backwards, pushing hard with my arms and the strong headwind it was all my weaker than usual legs, especially my right leg, could do to keep going, to keep pushing up the steep hill and not quit. My face was also freezing in the wind. It took everything I had to make it to the top of the hill, and I wondered if I could climb the last hill, especially if I had to continue to fight the strong headwind. I took a thirty second breather, but it was too cold in the strong wind to stand around and I started skinning up the gradual slope to the last hill. It has a longer and steeper lower half. Two thirds of the way up the slope, it becomes more gradual and then the top third becomes steeper. The wind was still blowing but not as strong. I put my head down and started counting steps rather than looking up to see how far I had to go. After what seemed like a long time I made it to the top of the last hill, turned right and headed up the last few hundred feet of gradual slope to the lodge where I could take refuge from the wind. I looked at my watch and saw that it had taken me 1 hour and 26 minutes. The previous year it took me 1 hour and 15 minutes on average. I didn't care. I had skinned to the top under challenging circumstances, struggling against a bitter and strong headwind during the hardest parts of the climb and I hadn't quit. I was not a "sissybedwetter."

John Schlichte: Winter climb Mt. Timpanogas

In the past it was not uncommon for my friend John Schlichte and me to pass other skinners and be the first to the top. The many times I had skinned alone I also was often the first to the top. It was a personal challenge and here I was, the first to the top again. Eight months and two days after the injury.

My last surgery had removed the screw from my right SI joint just six weeks before and a few weeks after that I was doubting that I would be able to skin to the top of the ski resort before the end of February. I felt incredibly grateful as I stood all alone by the lodge, my headlights casting a double elliptical glow on the snow in front of me, my boots locked into the ski bindings, ready to ski down the mountain and knowing I had truly been blessed to make the climb on this beautiful, early winter morning. My faith had been truly tested during the past eight months and today I had been blessed with one of those blessings that lets you know you are not alone, and you can keep pushing forward through other of life's challenges and trials.

Today was a small glimpse into my life for the past eight months. There were good days and terrible days. I was pushed mentally, emotionally, physically, and spiritually harder than I thought I could bear at times. With the help of my faithful wife, all the ministering angels surrounding me in life, and I am sure on the other side of the veil as well and with the habits of pondering, praying, reading from the scriptures and other inspiring books I had developed while bedbound, I have been able to keep going. The most important key was alone time with my Heavenly Father, and I spent a lot of alone time with Him, especially during those 2 months when I was spending most of my time in bed. With all this help, gradually, just like my adventure skinning up to the top of the mountain this morning, I was able to conquer those mental, emotional, physical, and spiritual mountains one at a time, hour by hour, day by day and month by month. Do I still have an uphill climb as my recovery continues? I believe so. As it said in the third priesthood blessing, "I would heal and on the other side of this trial I would learn lessons." I have learned many lessons and believe there are many more to learn.

For those of you who stuck it out and have read to this point and who may be struggling with major challenges in life, I would like to share some of what I feel are my most important insights gained from this trial.

Pelvic Fracture Journal entry 6/11/2021

I don't like this trial but my early morning routine of pondering, earnest prayer, reading scriptures and then from other religious books is a blessing and the calm in the eye of the storm. Personal quiet time is so necessary, and it is my lifeline as I go through this trial with its ups and downs, spiritual and physical highs and lows. I have learned more deeply that we must set aside quiet time to pray, ponder and study scriptures and good books. The world and social media should not be our God.

There were so many times I felt alone during the dark nights when I couldn't sleep. There were so many times I thought, "I can't take this pain." Many times, the doubt and despair were so powerful, making me want to give up. Somewhere along the way, I made some especially important and almost subconscious decisions. I chose to be grateful early on. The more I was grateful, the more I said thank you to those that helped me, it seems the more positive they were towards me. It also allowed me to be aware of the many blessings and miracles both great and small that Heavenly Father was blessing me with either directly or through ministering angels. I chose to follow President Uchtdorf's council to "Lift where you stand" or in my case "where I was lying". As I forgot myself and tried to serve others, I felt better, mentally, and spiritually. And finally, I chose to have faith. I chose to trust in all the prayers, the priesthood blessings, and the promises from the scriptures. I put my faith to the test, and I was not disappointed.

And finally, there were two habits I formed which allowed me to choose to be grateful, to serve and to have faith. The two habits that helped me the most through the difficulties, the highs and lows, the hope and despair: The first habit was setting aside quiet time to read from scriptures and other good books. The scripture verses, the thoughts and inspiring stories lifted my spirits. The second habit, which I believe was the most important, was setting aside alone time with my Heavenly Father to pray silently and many times vocally.

These habits helped me to not look down but to look up. I physically had to look up because I was confined to bed, but I also looked up mentally and spiritually, and that is where I found the hope and help to make it through this trial.

"I will lift up mine eyes unto the hills, from whence cometh my help". (Psalms 121:1)

Linda and Frank June 2022

Ready to not only look up but start climbing up again

Photos

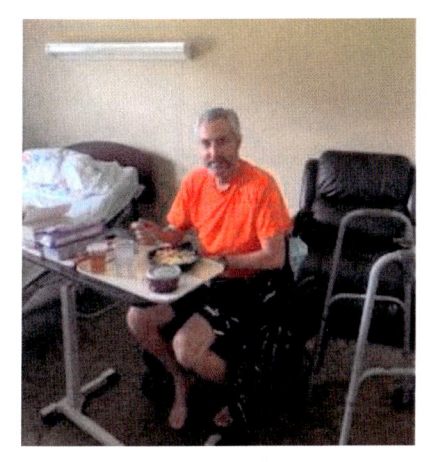

One of my first meals sitting up

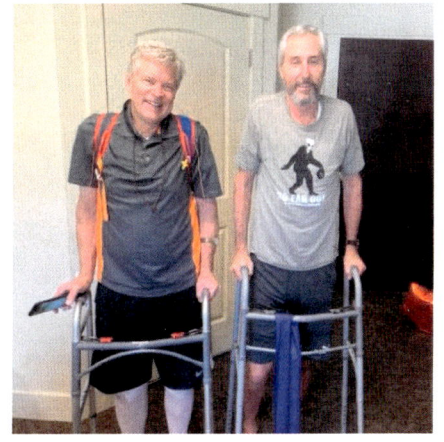

Friend Bob sharing a "walker" moment in care center

Staff members at Stone Henge care center

Weekend at Bear Lake during recovery

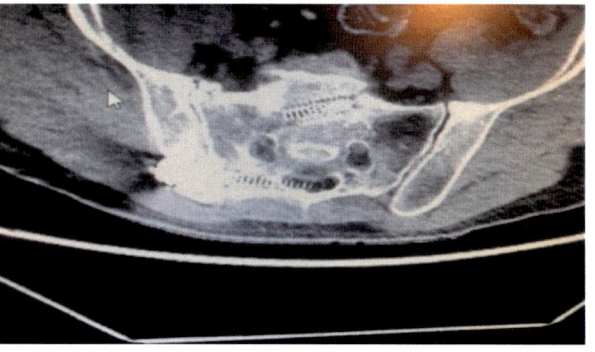

Handicap tag

CT scan image showing screw in the sacral spinal canal

Back to skinning again with Linda, Diane, and Blaine Austin February 2022

Blaine Austin, me, Rick Casteel April 2022

Frank on Chex. Picture taken at Warrior Rizen Ranch, Porterville Utah. Picture and horse courtesy of Al Petelinsek

Made in the USA
Columbia, SC
03 June 2025

5773e212-eaef-47bd-b5a8-ef1933a8bcccR01